Ms. Witt's book is a rare blend of scientific fact and practical wisdom. It stresses self-help for women dealing with premenstrual syndrome but will also aid in the understanding and application of medical therapy. I highly recommend this book.

Charles H. Debrovner, M.D.
Assistant Clinical Professor of
Obstetrics-Gynecology
New York University School of Medicine

This book can help women to understand more fully the physical, psychological, and sociological phenomena that constitute the premenstrual syndrome. It also has much to say to the physician caring for these women and certainly to families living with them. I recommend the book to all of you enthusiastically.

David S. Carroll, M.D.
Roosevelt Hospital
New York City

PMS: What Every Woman Should Know About Premenstrual Syndrome takes a well reasoned approach to a touchy problem. Much of the factual information provided will be of great value to women who are troubled by premenstrual symptoms. There are some really good self-help suggestions here! I found the coverage of the PMS clinics and progesterone therapy to be especially good—appropriately skeptical and cautious. Ms. Witt has done a fine job, and through the effort gone into this book she has made a useful contribution to the study of premenstrual syndrome.

Sharon Golub, Ph.D.
President
The Society for Menstrual Cycle
Research

PMS: What Every Woman Should Know About Premenstrual Syndrome filled me with hope about PMS, female sexuality, and women in general. This is an endorsement full of accolades.

Ms. Witt's positive approach to PMS is apparent throughout the book. The sections on female sexuality and orgasm as being positive self-help treatments for premenstrual tension are wonderful.

Another part that particularly appealed to me as founder and director of a PMS health care clinic, is the accent on "heightened awareness" and accent on "tapping into your inate creativity." While premenstrual . . . I'm using that in my interviews with patients and can see women's attitudes change right in front of my eyes. Those things we use to view as "working off steam or tension" become instead "creative outlets" and something we can do for ourselves when we're premenstrual. It makes me feel like we who have PMS are the fortunate ones, not those who don't. Making the emotional aspects of PMS a *positive* rather than a negative is the book's greatest accomplishment.

We are making this book available to our patients here at the Treatment Center. The staff and our patients are singing praises about *PMS: What Every Woman Should Know About Premenstrual Syndrome.*

This is a wonderful book. Ms. Witt has done good—for PMS, and for women.

Bonnie Jensen Oas, R.N.
Director
Women's Research and
    Treatment Center
Milford, New Hampshire

PMS demystifies this complex multi-determined condition called premenstrual syndrome and presents invaluable biological and medical information to the countless women who feel immobilized by its symptoms during "that time of the month." More importantly, it offers reassurance and hope and encourages women to feel more in control by helping them to identify symptoms and relieve many of them through nutrition and exercise. *PMS* should be read by all women.

Jeannine Masterson Michael, MSW, CSW
Director of Counseling
Eastern Women's Center
New York City

This is a terrific book! It's comprehensive and thorough about *everything* a woman should know on the subject. Ms. Witt takes premenstrual symptoms seriously while overcoming the image of women as helpless and hapless victims of their anatomy.

Barbara Sommer, Ph.D.
Department of Psychology
University of California

Reni L. Witt is a writer specializing in medical and related social issues. For this book, she has brought together the most important discoveries from recent medical and scientific research and from her interviews with gynecologists, endocrinologists, psychologists, nutritionists, and counselors. She also conducted in-depth interviews with women experiencing different levels of PMS problems. A frequent guest on television and radio talk shows and news programs across the country, Ms. Witt lives with her husband in Westchester County, New York.

By the same author:

MOM, I'M PREGNANT

Reni L. Witt with Jeannine Masterson Michael

PMS

What Every Woman Should Know About Premenstrual Syndrome

UPDATED

RENI L. WITT

STEIN AND DAY/*Publishers*/New York

FIRST STEIN AND DAY PAPERBACK EDITION 1984
PMS was first published in hardcover by
Stein and Day/*Publishers* in 1983 and has been updated for this edition

Copyright © 1983, 1984 by Reni L. Witt and Larimi Communications
All rights reserved, Stein and Day, Incorporated
Designed by Judith E. Dalzell
Printed in the United States of America
STEIN AND DAY/*Publishers*
Scarborough House
Briarcliff Manor, N.Y. 10510
ISBN 0-8128-8078-1

Contents

Acknowledgments

My sincere thanks to Michael M. Smith who introduced the idea for this book and whose support and guidance throughout its writing and final production are most valued.

I'd also like to express my deep appreciation to my publishers, Sol Stein and Patricia Day, who recognized the need for an overview on premenstrual syndrome based on reason and reality rather than the sea of sensationalism usually surrounding this issue.

Elizabeth Kelly edited the manuscript. I value her continued encouragement and literary guidance. Patricia Day supervised the project from its inception and I am grateful for her caring review of the work.

Women from across the nation participated in this book; portions of some of their interviews appear between these covers. (Their names have been changed to insure their privacy.) My heartfelt thanks to those who opened their lives, candidly revealing self-doubts, personal hurts, frustration, and confusion as a result of the depression, tension, anxiety, and physical pain that so often accompany the premenstrual phase. I am deeply grateful to all the women who shared this intimate part of their lives.

This book could not have been written without the information provided by many professional people who gave generously of their time and knowledge.

My special thanks to Dr. John Money, Ph.D., Professor of Medical Psychology at Johns Hopkins University in Baltimore, who provided me with much information regarding the theories concerning the causes of PMS, the relationship between psychology and the experience of the symptoms, sexual feelings during the premenstruum, and the role of progesterone in reducing violent impulses.

I would also like to express my thanks to Dr. Martin Weisberg, M.D., a respected gynecologist in private practice in Philadelphia, Pennsylvania, for relating his expertise regarding the various treatments for PMS, his knowledge of prescription medicines as they relate to the symptoms, as well as his insights into progesterone therapy and the PMS clinics.

I appreciate the assistance of Robert Plunkett and Romona Scheible of Science Editors, Inc., publishers of *Clin-Alert* for tracking down the side effects associated with the prescription drugs mentioned in this book.

Thanks also to Don LePone and Dean Siegal of Thompson Medical Company for their suggestions on over-the-counter treatments.

To Dr. Sharon Golub, Ph.D., President of the Society for Menstrual Cycle Research and Associate Professor of Psychology at the College of New Rochelle in New York, I extend my respectful appreciation for her research into the effects of PMS on performance, especially her perceptive comments about women's self-image and self-expectations during the premenstrual phase.

I am also most grateful for the research carried out by Dr. Barbara Sommer, Ph.D., of the Department of Psychology at the University of California. She provided much valuable information on the actual role of hormones on behavior and cognitive reasoning, as well as insights into the sociology of PMS, particularly the myths associated with the menstrual cycle and how these negative attitudes are integrated by women.

Roger Eastep, Supervisory Consumer Safety Officer for the Metabolic and Endocrine Drugs Division of the Food and Drug Administration, was very helpful in providing information about ormone treatment for PMS, particularly progesterone, and the ractices of many PMS clinics that prescribe progesterone.

I was in contact with several of these clinics and wish to cknowledge them, their founders and staff, all of whom sent nformation and some of whom spent many hours in interview: ames and Donna Hovey of the National Center for Premenstrual yndrome and Menstrual Distress, Inc., in New York; Carol Siegal f the PMS Program, Inc., and Jody Du Puis of APMS, Inc., in Massachusetts; Dawn Steinhofer of PMS Action, Inc., in Wisconin; Patti Cannon of the Rocky Mountain PMS Society, Inc., in Utah; and Lindsay Leckie of the National PMS Society, Inc., in North Carolina.

My thanks to Denise Copper and Donna Shubert of Women's Action Alliance and Barbara Whitney of Sex Information and Education Council of the United States for their references.

In addition, I'd like to thank Amy Frey of the K. D. McCormick Library at Planned Parenthood, World Population Office, in Manhattan. Her competent assistance was invaluable in locating medical journals and textbooks as well as other books and literature pertaining to this subject. My thanks also to the library staff of the New York Academy of Medicine for allowing me to use their facilities.

Odette de la Tour provided the illustrations and graphs found in the book. Her talents are much appreciated.

Thanks to Beej Johnson and Barbara Weiss who assisted me in the research, and my special appreciation to Nancy McDonald who encouraged me while typing and retyping the manuscript. My thanks also to Karen Devoti for her secretarial support and sunny smile.

Finally, loving thanks to my husband, Jeffrey W. Kriz, who cheers me up and lends his shoulder during "that time of the month" and throughout the months and years.

Reni L. Witt
New York City

Foreword

After reading *PMS . . . What Every Woman Should Know About Premenstrual Syndrome,* I am moved to congratulate the author on another fine work. As in Reni Witt's previous book, *Mom, I'm Pregnant,* she has reached a specific audience with needs that have not heretofore been adequately addressed. And she has achieved these goals so well that I think the book will provide significant help for the millions of women who live with the symptoms of PMS in ignorance, pain, guilt, and shame.

Specifically, the writing is clear, to the point, and in language that makes a complex subject easily understandable to the reading audience. The book is comprehensive and sober. Not only is every aspect of PMS thoroughly discussed, but I am impressed by the inclusion of virtually every theory of causation, interpretation, and treatment. It's all presented in a calm, dispassionate manner, which should enable the reader to identify her own unique pattern and make truly informed decisions about her personal welfare. In fact, the knowledge presented and the repeated emphasis on self-awareness should help the reader acquire more of a sense of control over her life in general. The reader will inevitably come away with more knowledge.

The book is sympathetic and supportive. (How many women have, in a lifetime, craved that kind of support?) But it doesn't stop there. While independent "validation" of one's personal experience may be very helpful, the inclusion of a discussion of many positive aspects of PMS could be genuinely therapeutic. This touch is indicative of the care that has gone into the preparation of this book.

Other points that have impacted on me include:

1. The most comprehensive description I've read of women's variations and experiences with their menstrual cycles. It was illuminating to me and I am a physician already sensitive to women's issues.
2. Given a specific set of premenstrual symptoms, the book enables the reader to determine the most likely causes.
3. The advised remedies are sound, complete, and presented in a suggested hierarchy, going from simple to complex, while encouraging the reader to stay with the simplest method that succeeds. This is in keeping with good medical practice.
4. Since there is much variation in physicians' knowledge of PMS, this book prepares the reader to become a true partner in her own health care and should insure that such care will be of improved quality.

In conclusion, I think that this book will not only fill a great gap in the health literature, but it's so well done that it could positively alter the lives of most women with PMS. Given the prediction that the 1980's will see a breakthrough in PMS recognition and care, this book could be one of the most important of those breakthroughs.

Harvey W. Caplan, M.D.
American Society of
Sex Educators, Counselors and
Therapists (A.S.S.E.C.T.)
San Francisco, California

Preface

Beneath the stormy sea so often pictured with premenstrual syndrome, lies the fundamental issue of self-control. The perceived lack of control over bodily and emotional changes taking place during the menstrual cycle is the foundation of much controversy, confusion, and concern over PMS.

Premenstrual syndrome is said to cause everything from moodiness to madness to murder. The media have become inundated with sensationalist accounts of frenzied females, powerless against the surging tides of their raging hormones.

What is PMS and just what is its effect on women?

To begin, premenstrual syndrome is not a disease; it shouldn't be a stigma; and it's not even a true syndrome. A syndrome is defined as a group of symptoms occurring together, producing a pattern consistent from individual to individual that is predictable and typical of a particular disease. In other words, one person with tuberculosis, diabetes, or pneumonia will display the same symptoms, development, and outcome of the disease as any other person with tuberculosis, diabetes, or pneumonia.

PMS is different. The symptoms vary from woman to woman and progress unpredictably in any individual woman over the months and years. This does not mean premenstrual syndrome is psychogenic or nonexistent, but rather that the word "syndrome" is not an accurate description.

PMS might be better described as a "condition," a more general term reflecting bodily and emotional changes common to most women prior to menstruation and not necessarily implying disease or ailment.

But whether it is called premenstrual condition, premenstrual syndrome, premenstrual tension, congestive dysmenorrhea, a medical chamelean, the male chauvinist's revenge, or the "Kitchen sink syndrome" (since it's been associated with everything but), there is a great deal of new information about which every woman should know. In fact, this book might have been subtitled "Good News About Premenstrual Syndrome."

- Women do not have to suffer bloating, headaches, breast pain, irritability, tension, depression, and other symptoms that occur before menstruation.
- Women need no longer think they are emotionally unstable, "going crazy," hormonally inferior, or "all alone" when premenstrual changes take place.
- The myths surrounding the monthly changes are giving way to medical revelations and renewed respect for women's ability to cope with premenstrual changes.
- The existence of PMS does not have to be used against the advances made by women in this society.
- Doctors and researchers are closing in on the causes of premenstrual syndrome, especially in its severe form.
- Every woman can learn basic premenstrual health management to help ease the numerous symptoms.
- It's possible to overcome most premenstrual symptoms without expensive prescription medicines.
- For women with extremely severe PMS, new medical advances and treatments are now available.
- PMS even has a positive side, one that science has yet barely explored.
- Women with PMS are not helpless. They can take control over this part of their lives.

Nowhere in this book are women referred to as "PMS victims."

The word victim comes from the Latin and means "to have been conquered." On the contrary, women are learning how to gain control over their symptoms, demanding serious medical attention, encouraging further scientific research, and, in the process, are starting to conquer PMS—and that's very good news, indeed.

1

THAT TIME OF THE MONTH

What Is Premenstrual Syndrome?

Ten days before my period starts, I begin to have the symptoms. I feel depressed, hopeless, paranoid, bitchy. Physically, I become very tense. My muscles are tight, especially around my shoulders, neck, and upper back. I feel cramps and my legs get spasms. The worst part is feeling out of control of my life. Some people seem to cope with mood swings. Maybe they're just more relaxed about their emotions. But being in control of myself is terribly important to me.

Alice M., 36
Social worker

What Is Premenstrual Syndrome?

It happens about once a month—during *that* time of the month. You may notice your favorite slacks won't zip up. Some days it's impossible to slip a ring on or off your finger. You drop things or feel clumsy. You might initiate an argument with a loved one, only to think afterward, "What was that all about?" There may be days when you feel like crying without end. A persistent headache that aspirin won't stop keeps you in blinding pain for days. You may experience the anguish of having to avoid your children's hugs because your breasts hurt so much. You feel alarm at your own sudden violent impulses.

And you wonder, "Is there something wrong with me? Why am I losing control of myself?"

If you have ever felt this way during that time of the month, you are not alone.

All healthy women have monthly menstrual cycles and almost every woman experiences feelings that indicate to her menstruation will soon take place. Various surveys have shown that up to 95 percent of women report feeling some physical and/or psychological changes that occur during the days and weeks before the onset of the menstrual flow. It is believed that women all over the world experience these monthly changes.

For some women, these changes are mild. They may be barely

noticeable. For other women, between 20 percent and 60 percent the changes are numerous and range from moderate to severe These uncomfortable, and often disquieting, feelings may affec some facets of their day-to-day lives. For approximately 5 percent t 10 percent of these women, however, the four to fourteen day before menstruation are a time of intense pain, frustration, and despair. Normal life activities can be interrupted by severe de pression, irrational mood swings, temporary paralysis, periodi asthma, and even epilepsy.

There is a name for the wide variety of bodily and emotiona feelings, changes, or symptoms that occur before menstruation. I is called premenstrual syndrome, or PMS.

Premenstrual syndrome is not the pain, such as cramps, asso ciated with actual menstruation. Rather, it is an extremely comple: condition, involving physical and psychological symptoms tha appear *before* menstruation begins and end with the onset of th monthly flow. Women who suffer from PMS notice that thei symptoms begin anywhere from two days to two weeks befor menstruation. The start of menstrual bleeding usually brings relie from the symptoms, which do not reappear again until it is onc more the two to fourteen days before menstruation. Thus the PM! cycle repeats itself in tandem with the menstrual cycle.

There are several theories as to how and why this takes place Although as yet no one element has been found to cause th multiple symptoms of PMS, it is believed that premenstrual syn drome has a biochemical origin, but is also influenced by psycho logical and social factors. These theories will be explored mor fully in the following chapters.

You may be experiencing some of the puzzling changes that are part of premenstrual syndrome. In this next section, we'll take look at some of the major physical and psychological symptom that may be affecting you during that time of the month.

The Symptoms of PMS

There are many different feelings or changes associated with premenstrual syndrome. Over seventy symptoms have been com piled by various doctors and gynecologists. You may have experienced any number of them. Some women have only one or two symptoms. Others experience ten or more simultaneously or sequentially. Sometimes, the symptoms can be quite severe; other times, they are hardly noticed. In addition, some women's symptoms change from month to month, while other women have the same ones every month. The intensity of the symptoms can vary with each menstrual cycle. The symptoms can also change over the lifetime of a woman and can be triggered by childbirth, surgery, or trauma.

Probably no two women experience PMS in exactly the same way. Again, PMS is not so much *what* the symptoms are, but *when* they occur.

Although PMS can affect the central nervous system, cardiovascular system, gastrointestinal system, metabolism, muscles, genitals, emotions, and moods, for general purposes these symptoms can be divided into two categories—physical and psychological.

The Physical Symptoms of PMS

One of the major complaints women express during the premenstrual period is bloating, or water retention. This can result in breast swelling and/or tenderness, swollen feet, ankles, fingers, wrists, and abdomen. Some women feel bloated all over. Some notice a weight gain of several pounds during that time. A few swell to five, ten, even twenty pounds above their normal weight. Water retention may be responsible for a host of other related PMS symptoms, including headaches and migraines, not to mention the edginess and irritability that come with physical discomfort from bloating.

Other common symptoms associated with PMS include constipation or diarrhea, nausea and an aversion to food, or an increased appetite, especially for sweets or salty foods.

Some women feel the need to urinate frequently while others notice they can "drink gallons of water and never have to go to the bathroom." Unquenchable thirst combined with a decrease in urine output is a common PMS symptom.

21

In the week before her menstrual period starts, a woman may feel an increased desire for alcoholic drinks. Some women turn to drinking for relief from the discomfort or tension they feel premenstrually. Ironically, in the days before menstruation, the female body reaches a significantly higher blood alcohol level than at any other time in the cycle. You may have noticed that alcohol affects you differently at different times of the month. A woman who is accustomed to a cocktail before dinner or to several glasses of wine with a meal may feel surprisingly high or tipsy after the first drink.

Other frequently reported physical symptoms include aching joints, muscle tension or cramps, and backaches. Many women get "period pimples" or an outbreak of acne. Vaginal discharge and uterine cramping are also commonly experienced during that time of the month.

The Psychological Symptoms of PMS

A wide range of psychological changes also take place during the premenstruum (the period of time before the onset of menstruation).

One of the most common is the feeling of tension. That tense feeling may manifest itself physically—for example, headaches and muscle stiffness—but can also lead to emotional symptoms such as nervousness, edginess, and irritability.

Because this feeling is one of the most common symptoms, PMS is still often referred to as premenstrual tension, or PMT. Indeed, tension does describe the mental, emotional, or nervous strain many women feel premenstrually.

For other women, the most pronounced feeling is one of lethargy. Some women report feeling sluggish, drowsy, forgetful, apathetic, or a loss of vigor.

Yet another symptom often associated with PMS is depression. Depression may take the form of "feeling on the verge of tears," decreased self-confidence and self-esteem, or thoughts of suicide.

To the woman suffering from depression, this can seem like the most serious symptom and the one most difficult to overcome. Women who experience premenstrual depression often report a vere loss of self-esteem. They feel they are not useful or valued. metimes, a woman can feel that everybody is against her, that she all alone in the world. She may think her life and her future are thout hope.

Although the depressed feelings most often disappear once menruation starts, those days of despair are difficult to cope with. To ake matters worse, it is possible for a woman to worry afterward at she might be losing her mind, that she is going insane or coming schizophrenic. Unless there is an understanding of this articular symptom of PMS, a woman can develop profound lf-doubt.

There are other psychological symptoms associated with preenstrual syndrome. They include anxiety, paranoia, mood vings, sleep disorders, and hostility. Depending on their intensity, ese feelings can cause anguish and confusion, as well as conflict d misunderstanding with loved ones. PMS affects you most rectly, but it can also affect those people who are most important your life.

Is There a Positive Side to PMS?

Premenstrual syndrome is most often described in terms of negave symptoms, but in the week before menstruation a substantial umber of women do report having several positive feelings. The ositive aspects that are most frequently associated with PMS clude:

- increased sexual drive
- increased feelings of well-being
- increased creativity

Some women say they experience a burst of energy. They feel like king bread or doing extra cleaning during the days before menruation starts.

As one woman joked, "If it wasn't for PMS, my house would ver get cleaned."

It is possible to feel some of the more severe physical symptoms while experiencing a sense of increased self-confidence. For example, a woman may have painful, swollen breasts, yet feel a surge of confidence in the face of a stressful situation.

Of course, women who have positive feelings premenstrually usually do not have any reason to report these "symptoms" to the doctor. Therefore, less is known about this aspect of PMS. As it is the women who bake an extra batch of cookies for their children, or write poetry, or perform well on the job during the premenstruum do not, unfortunately, make headlines.

Society and Premenstrual Syndrome

For better or worse, it is the most negative and sensational aspect of PMS that have made the news.

For better, because this has stimulated interest that may promote further research into the causes and treatments of premenstrual syndrome.

For worse, because false assumptions are made. The thinking goes along these lines: because relatively few women experience debilitating symptoms or display bizarre behavior premenstrually, *all* women do. One man's comment following the English murder cases involving PMS illustrates this point: "Since those two women committed murder right before their periods, does that mean all women are capable of killing during that time of the month?"

This question underlies much of the controversy surrounding premenstrual syndrome and may weigh as heavily on the average woman as any bodily or emotional symptom.

PMS has been blamed for everything from moodiness to madness to murder. The syndrome has been used to explain emotional instability, child abuse, and violent crime. It has been used to justify preventing women from attaining positions of power in business and politics. ("We can't have a woman President! Suppose she pushes The Button during That Time of the Month?" The answer: "What if a man pushes The Button during a fit of macho bravura?" Throughout history, it is men who have instigated the world's worst wars and holocausts and have dominated entire nations through oppression and dictatorship. Women may have PMS once a month—what do men have all month long?)

At the same time that PMS is considered real enough to cause a myriad of social ills, it is also said to be "all in a woman's mind." Throughout the years, various physicians and psychiatrists have claimed that premenstrual syndrome was caused by neurosis, emotional disturbance, a hysterical personality, a hostile mother-daughter relationship, rejection of the feminine role, and even penis envy.

In spite of medical advances in the knowledge of the menstrual cycle and PMS, women are still being told by some doctors and others that the symptoms are imaginary, that this is a means to manipulate others, or that PMS is merely psychosomatic. It is interesting to observe that these same excuses were used to dismiss menstrual cramping and pain, which were also thought to be imaginary or psychosomatic.

These attitudes permeate a woman's conscience and influence her self-perception, which in turn can worsen some PMS symptoms. The social stigma surrounding menstruation and premenstrual syndrome can prevent a woman from seeking the help and support she needs to overcome her cyclical symptoms. Many women, perhaps you, have felt some shame or embarrassment about having the symptoms of PMS.

In chapter 7 of this book we'll take a closer look at how cultural values affect women who have PMS, examine what's behind the highly charged issue of murder and madness as it relates to PMS, and reveal several fascinating studies that shed new light on PMS and performance on the job.

Why Has So Little Been Done?

No matter what is said about premenstrual syndrome, the reality is that millions of women experience its symptoms every month. If so many women, indeed, so many people, are experiencing a certain set of symptoms on a regular, recurring basis, why has so little been done? More than one caring gynecologist has asked, "How can millions be spent on research for some obscure disease that affects only a few thousand individuals, while almost nothing has been done about a condition that affects almost half the population?"

The sociology of PMS is one contributing factor. As mentioned, some doctors continue to doubt that PMS is real. It seems like a chameleon condition. There are so many diverse symptoms. They come and go. Taken individually, the symptoms can occur at any time of the month. Most are common to both men and women. They may also be indicative of many other conditions, diseases, or psychological problems. The variety and changeability of the symptoms make controlled scientific studies difficult to perform. Many doctors and psychologists admit that the only real evidence for PMS is the reports of women who experience the symptoms. Without concrete proof, it is too easy to dismiss PMS as imaginary.

A second related reason why so little real information has been available is the general lack of attention paid by the medical community to the reality of women's complaints.

Too many doctors have said something to the effect of "There, there, it's not so bad. You'll just have to learn how to live with it." Or "It's all in your head. See a psychiatrist." Or even "You're trying too hard to make it in a man's world. You have to accept yourself as a woman."

In addition, many doctors did not see PMS as a serious enough condition to warrant major research. After all, no one has ever died of PMS (although some women may feel like dying during that time!).

Men do not have menstrual cycles and, on the whole, do not identify with women who have discomfort or pain associated with menstruation. In the past, most physicians and medical researchers were men, many of whom would candidly admit that PMS is simply not that interesting to them. (One has to wonder if the same set of symptoms were occurring monthly, say to 40 percent of men, whether the condition would not suddenly become more intriguing.) Furthermore, the decisions to provide financial grants to support medical research are made by universities, corporations, and/or the government, all of which are still primarily headed by men.

In fairness, there are doctors and researchers who have recognized the significance of the symptoms reported by women who came to them seeking relief. Many physicians have attempted to alleviate the symptoms, some with more success than others; however, so little research has been carried out in this area that a physician may be unsure what treatment might work best and most consistently. Chances are your doctor received little or no training in diagnosing or treating premenstrual syndrome. Some gynecological textbooks currently used in medical schools do not even mention PMS.

This may all change in the near future. Social changes and recent developments have created renewed interest in the search for causes and treatment of PMS.

PMS—the Most Important Women's Health Issue of the Decade

Five years ago, most people had never even heard of premenstrual syndrome, even though women have probably suffered from it since the dawn of humanity. Now, suddenly, PMS is being heralded as the most important women's health issue of the 80s. Medical and popular interest in this field has blossomed seemingly overnight. PMS clinics are opening up in various states around the nation. Self-help groups have sprung up in many communities. Television shows and magazine articles have featured stories on PMS.

What happened? Why now?

There are several closely related reasons why attention is now being given to discovering the cause and the treatment of premenstrual syndrome. One of the most important is the liberation of sexual information that opened up the discussion and knowledge about menstruation and premenstrual syndrome. Such free discussion about women's monthly cycles was always considered taboo. Even in the recent past, just ten to fifteen years ago, it was almost impossible even to mention menstruation, let alone discuss it in mixed company. (It is still taboo in many families and social circles.)

Women, therefore, bore their aches, pains, and cramps alone and in silence. And it was all too easy to dismiss these discomforts as imaginary.

All of this began to change in 1931, when Dr. Robert T. Frank read, at a meeting of the Section of Neurology and Psychiatry of the New York Academy of Medicine, his paper describing the hormonal causes of premenstrual tension. His was the first attempt to describe scientifically the symptoms that affected a large group of his patients during the premenstrual period.

Then, in 1953, Dr. Katharina Dalton, of the University College Hospital in London, England, published a major paper that appeared in a British medical journal. Her paper was based on the clinical research she had been doing since 1948 on premenstrual tension. It was her work that caused the general medical community to become aware of PMS. Although her theories and treatments, which will be discussed later in this book, continue to generate controversy and criticism, she has contributed a great deal to our current awareness of premenstrual syndrome.

In the early 60s another medical event took place that reshaped our ideas about sexual pleasure and women's role in society—and led to some amazing discoveries about the menstrual cycle.

That event was the widespread marketing and acceptance of the birth control pill. The Pill made a woman biologically free. No longer did she have to fear an unwanted pregnancy as a result of sexual intimacy. Reproductively speaking, woman became equal to man—that is, he didn't have to worry about getting pregnant, now neither did she.

That simple fact helped to fertilize the ground for the 1960s sexual revolution and the 1970s women's liberation movement. The women's movement spurred on the medical self-help concept and the demand for patient's rights. As a result, the doctor-patient relationship changed profoundly. People now feel they have the right to question their doctor in order to receive the best health care possible. Many women are actively seeking doctors who understand PMS, and some are starting their own self-help organizations with other women to find the health care and support needed. Such individuals and groups have encouraged a demand for research into the causes and treatments of PMS.

In addition to the dramatic social changes caused in great part by the Pill, a fascinating and unexpected observation was made.

The Pill seemed to stop menstrual pain. For millions of women on the Pill, cramps disappeared or were greatly alleviated. When they went off the Pill, the monthly pain returned. Back on the Pill, the pain vanished.

As women described to their gynecologists their relief from menstrual cramps, doctors began to prescribe the Pill specifically for menstrual distress with very positive results.

For the first time, the medical community began to recognize what millions of women have known for countless centuries— menstrual pain is real. There is a physical cause, and just recently the most likely cause for the pain was discovered. Scientific evidence strongly suggests menstrual pain is caused by a natural hormone-like substance called prostaglandins. Anti-prostaglandin medications have been developed and are being found very effective in relieving intense menstrual pain. Some doctors theorize that prostaglandins may also be responsible for many PMS symptoms.

Current interest in premenstrual syndrome is a result of the success found in treating menstrual pain. Since it must now be acknowledged by the medical community that menstrual pain has an identifiable source, it can no longer be dismissed as the "hysterical complaints of idle women." It is real.

PMS may very well be proven real in the same manner in the very near future.

What Can I Do Right Now about PMS?

Doctors and counselors who work with PMS patients agree that the first step in overcoming PMS is to recognize it. Many women who have the symptoms don't even realize that what they are going through every month has a name. Other women are not sure whether their feelings are really a part of PMS or something else.

The next chapter will help you to identify the symptoms of PMS and will show you how you can determine whether or not your symptoms are related to your monthly cycle. If you do have PMS, this book will tell you how you can help yourself right now.

Learning about her monthly cycles is also important to any woman who wants to feel like herself again every week of the month. Chapters 3 and 4 will take a look at the hormonal workings of the female body as well as explore the various theories concerning the causes of PMS.

Chapters 5 through 7 will examine in detail the particular symptoms of PMS. By understanding the possible causes for the symptoms that trouble you most, you can better help yourself and/or work with a doctor to find a way to ease the pain.

A great deal of knowledge has been gathered for this book in order to help women help themselves to overcome PMS. Suggestions include diet, exercise, sex, and certain over-the-counter medications that have provided relief for countless women.

Doctors and clinics specializing in PMS treatments can also provide pharmaceutical ways to help women, especially those women whose PMS symptoms are severe. Although some of the prescription treatments offered are controversial, many women have found them to be the solution to the intense pain they suffer during that time of the month. You'll read how some women have been able to return to normal lives again after using these new medications and you'll be provided with a guide to the benefits and the risks discovered so far in these medical advances.

Finally, we'll take a look at the many ways to successfully cope with premenstrual syndrome in every part of your daily life.

2

DO YOU HAVE PREMENSTRUAL SYNDROME?

How to Find Out

For twenty-five years, I have believed there was something wrong with me. Some weeks, I'd feel so blue and irritable. I couldn't cope with anything. I'd scream at my children, pick fights with my husband, throw things, drink too much, anything to escape from the terrible tension. Then this mood would pass and I would vow never to behave like that again. Until next time. Then, after watching a TV program about PMS, I started keeping a chart. It turned out that my black moods began regularly about ten days before my period started.

Brenda P., 48
Housewife

Do You Have PMS?—
Fifteen Ways to Find Out

The first step in overcoming premenstrual syndrome is to determine whether you have it. This sounds simple enough, yet in reality many women suffer the most severe symptoms without realizing they have PMS.

Unfortunately, there is no blood test or gynecological examination that can tell you or your doctor if you have premenstrual syndrome. Because of the complexity of this condition, even a gynecologist can easily misdiagnose premenstrual syndrome. Should PMS be mistaken for another condition or disease, the resulting treatment can be ineffective or may actually worsen the symptoms. Countless women who have sought medical help for their monthly pain report doctors' diagnoses of anything from tumors to manic depression. Treatments have run the gamut from tranquilizers to hysterectomies, both of which, incidentally, can exacerbate an existing condition of premenstrual syndrome.

Therefore, it is extremely important that a careful study of your symptoms be made before you accept treatment such as prescriptive medicines, hormone therapy, or gynecological surgery.

There is good news, though. Most women who suffer from PMS diagnose their own condition. You, too, can determine for yourself whether your symptoms are related to your menstrual cycle. And if they are, you can find relief.

The following general questions can help you begin to find ou whether you have premenstrual syndrome. Circle your response usually — U; sometimes — S; rarely — R.

1) Do you ever have backaches or muscle tension around your shoulders and neck just before your period?   U   S   R

2) Do your breasts ever feel tender or swollen, or do they feel fibrous or lumpy in the week or so before the start of your period?   U   S   R

3) Do you ever feel bloated or do you gain several pounds before the onset of your period?   U   S   R

4) Do you ever feel like crying or are you depressed several days before your period starts?   U   S   R

5) Do you ever feel cramping several days before the start of actual menstrual bleeding?   U   S   R

6) Would you describe the pain you have during your period as less severe than the pain and discomfort before?   U   S   R

7) Do you ever have headaches or migraines before menstruation begins?   U   S   R

8) Do you ever feel nervous, tense, or irritable before your period begins?   U   S   R

9) Do your symptoms seem to recur regularly?   U   S   R

10) Does the start of your period bring relief from your symptoms?   U   S   R

11) Do you ever have several symptoms at once?   U   S   R

12) Is there a period of time every month when you are symptom-free?   U   S   R

13) Do you ever feel tired or lethargic before your period?   U   S   R

14) Do you ever get cravings for salty or sweet
    foods premenstrually?   U   S   R
15) If you have headaches or other symptoms
    throughout the month, are they worse
    right before your period?   U   S   R

If you answer usually or sometimes to most of these questions,
you probably have premenstrual syndrome. But how can you be
sure?

Diagnosing PMS

How can you tell whether the discomfort and pain you feel once
a month are due to premenstrual syndrome or to something else? As
already mentioned, PMS is a chameleon condition—it is often
believed to be something else. Women themselves wonder if there is
an organic cause for their symptoms, such as cancer. Or they worry
that the problem lies with a disease in the reproductive system. Or
they fear that they are "going insane." In any case, feeling out of
control during that time of the month is a common experience for
many women.

Doctors who treat women with PMS agree that in the vast
majority of cases, there is no physical disease or disorder causing
the symptoms. Furthermore, serious mental disturbances that can
cause PMS-like symptoms are rare.

It is, however, probably a good idea to have a routine physical
and/or gynecological checkup to rule out any organic cause for
your symptoms.

You can work with your doctor to diagnose PMS, but most
women are able to identify this condition by themselves, using the
guidelines presented in this chapter.

Let's take a look at the four significant elements in diagnosing
PMS—*who* can have the condition, *what* the symptoms are, *where*
they take place in the body, and *when* they occur.

Who Has PMS?

Almost all women have some kind of discomfort around the time of menstruation. Doctors use the medical term dysmenorrhea (pronounced dis-men-o-ree-a) to describe the discomfort or pain associated with the menstrual process. There are two types of dysmenorrhea. For the purposes of diagnosing and treating PMS, it is important to distinguish between them.

At least 80 percent of women suffer from some degree of pain, or cramps, *during* their menstrual period. This type of pain is properly called "spasmodic dysmenorrhea," which accurately reflects the spasms of pain and cramping felt during the first day or so of menstrual bleeding. Most women who have spasmodic dysmenorrhea remember having it since their early teens. It is possible for this pain to continue once a month until menopause; however, its intensity often diminishes with age. In many cases, the pain of spasmodic dysmenorrhea seems to be reduced or disappears completely following childbirth. Birth-control pills also alleviate painful cramping during menstruation. Although this pain is obviously related to the menstrual cycle, it is not a part of PMS.

Approximately 40 percent of women have PMS to a degree ranging from moderate to severe. This condition can also be described medically as "congestive dysmenorrhea." Unlike menstrual cramping, the symptoms of congestive dysmenorrhea or PMS begin for most women during their mid to late twenties, although occasionally they begin during the teen years. Frequently, this condition progresses so gradually that a woman may be unaware that her symptoms are worsening as time goes by. Women can experience this pain throughout their reproductive lives, although it can vary greatly. For unknown reasons, the symptoms tend to increase in number and intensity with the passing years. Unfortunately, childbirth and birth-control pills sometimes exacerbate congestive dysmenorrhea or can even bring it on. (Pregnancy itself brings relief from PMS symptoms and, paradoxically, birth-control pills actually alleviate many premenstrual symptoms for some women.)

It was once theorized that a woman couldn't suffer from spasmodic *and* congestive dysmenorrhea. But too many women report experiencing both to validate this belief. It can be said, however, that a woman suffers *primarily* from one or the other.

For example, Jane M., 30, a stenographer, has some bloating, breast tenderness, and occasionally a headache before her period starts. But once her menstrual flow begins, the pain and cramping are so intense that she sometimes feels like fainting. On the first day of her period, she frequently cancels social engagements and often cannot go in to work. Jane suffers primarily from spasmodic dysmenorrhea.

On the other hand, Margie T., 34, a salesclerk and mother, suffers greatly during the week before her period starts. She feels horribly bloated, nauseated, has persistent diarrhea, and severe headaches. In addition, depression descends upon her, darkening her disposition as the days go by. Some months, on the day before her period, the depression becomes so severe she cannot pull herself out of bed. Once her period begins, she describes the feeling of "a cloud lifting off my shoulders." Margie has some menstrual cramping that she describes as "moderate, but it's nothing compared to the agony I go through *before* my period starts." Margie suffers primarily from congestive dysmenorrhea, or premenstrual syndrome.

Almost all women experience some degree of dysmenorrhea. Many suffer through both forms. It is the very rare woman who feels no discomfort at all around the time of menstruation.

Where PMS Takes Place in the Body

Understanding where the symptoms take place in the body can also help you to determine whether you have PMS.

First, let's examine where spasmodic dysmenorrhea is centered. Menstrual cramping is localized, involving the uterus, the lower abdomen, and the genital area. The pain can also radiate to the buttocks, lower back, and the inside of the upper thighs. Some have called this "bikini pain," since it basically covers the same area of the body as does a bikini.

Unlike spasmodic dysmenorrhea, premenstrual syndrome is not localized. Rather, the symptoms can include the whole body, and especially the breasts, abdomen, wrists, hands, ankles, and feet. Congestive dysmenorrhea also includes headache, backache, and joint stiffness; constipation or diarrhea; an increase or decrease of urine output; as well as fatigue, depression, irritability, and mood swings.

The drawing below can help you identify which dysmenorrhea affects you.

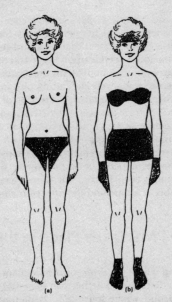

(a)   (b)

The shaded areas indicate parts of the body affected by spasmodic dysmenorrhea or menstrual cramping (a) and those affected by congestive dysmenorrhea or PMS (b).

A Complete List of PMS Symptoms

There are over seventy symptoms, both positive and negative, associated with premenstrual syndrome. Many are quite common. Others are relatively rare. The symptoms, or combination of symptoms, as well as their severity, vary with each individual woman.

Tension	Anxiety
Depression	Change in sexual drive
Irritability	Crying spells
Lethargy	Inner reflection
Melancholy	Fatigue
Thoughts of dying or suicide	Euphoria
Violent impulses	Feelings of well-being
Clumsiness or accident proneness	Increased creativity
Craving for alcohol	Bursts of energy
Feelings of panic	Rheumatism
Forgetfulness	Bloating or swelling
Mood swings	Increased body weight
Restlessness	Edema
Sleep problems	Styes
Vivid dreams	Conjunctivitis
Headaches	Glaucoma
Migraine	Sore throat
Fainting	Hoarseness
Vertigo	Cystitis
Epilepsy or seizures	Urethritis
Dizziness	Altered urinary output
Ringing in ears	Vaginal discharge
Tunnel vision	Abdominal congestion
Blind spots	Food cravings
Acne	Overeating or bingeing
Period pimples	Aversion to food
Boils	Nausea
Outbreak of herpes	Breast tenderness
Itching	Asthma

Sinusitis	Aching varicose veins
Backache	Chest pains
Joint pain	Rapid heartbeats
Bowel cramping	Constipation
Diarrhea	Thirst
Vomiting	Hypoglycemia
Hostility or anger	Hives
Fibrous, lumpy breasts	

Fortunately, no one woman could possibly have all these symptoms at the same time. Most women, though, experience several. You may recognize yourself as having many of the symptoms listed. It is important to remember that as diverse as these symptoms seem, there is a common denominator: if you have PMS, your symptoms will recur on a monthly cycle, just before your menstrual period begins.

When the Symptoms Occur

Probably the most important element in diagnosing PMS is its timing—that is, *when* the symptoms occur. For now, the best way to determine whether you have PMS is to keep a calendar or a chart with a daily recording of your symptoms as well as your menstrual cycle. This chart is necessary to see if a pattern emerges. This is a simple and effective method recommended by leading doctors and other experts who are skilled in diagnosing premenstrual syndrome.

To learn how to keep your chart, let's begin by taking a look at a chart kept by Judy W., 28, a registered nurse and the mother of two children.

Ever since the birth of her second child five years ago, Judy experienced periodic depression. Some days she cried uncontrollably. During this time, she often had trouble coping with her responsibilities at home and in the hospital. Judy also noticed how sore her breasts became and when she felt little lumps there, she panicked each time.

Judy describes her inner fears:

> *I didn't know what was wrong with me. All I knew was that once a month I lost control over my emotions and my body. During the weeks when I had no symptoms, I worried about being a bad mother, that I was neurotic or that I had cancer. So, really, there were no good days for me. I was either in pain and depressed or I was worried when it would happen again.*

An article about PMS that appeared in a woman's magazine prompted Judy to keep a chart of her symptoms. After only two months, a pattern began to emerge.

In January, her symptoms began on the ninth. They increased in intensity with each passing day. She had breast pain, bloatedness, and frequently started arguments with her husband. By the fourteenth, she had an excruciating headache that would not be relieved even by extra-strength headache tablets. She cried off and on all day. On the fifteenth, her period began and the headache disappeared. In fact, she felt cheerier than she had in over a week.

In February, her symptoms began around the sixth. Again, they steadily increased in number and severity until the thirteenth when she suffered another incapacitating headache. When her period started the next morning, she once again felt enormous physical and emotional relief.

Judy continued to record her symptoms for four months. Her results appear on the next pages.

By looking at her chart, Judy was able to make a clear connection between her menstrual periods and her symptoms. After realizing what was happening to her and when, she understood her symptoms were not random and not due to emotional instability. In fact, she now feels proud of herself for coping as well as she does during that difficult time of the month. *Knowing* when her symptoms will occur is helping her gain some control over her situation.

PMS MENSTRUAL CALENDAR

MONTH January

Sunday	Monday	Tuesday	Wednesday	Thursday	Friday	Saturday
					1	2
3	4	5	6	7	8	9 BP BLT FT CRY
10 BP FT CRY	11 BP BLT CRY	12 HD CMP BP CRY	13 HD CMP BP BLT	14 HD Thirst BP CRY	15 P	16 P
17 P	18 P	19 P	20	21	22	23
24	25	26	27	28	29	30
31						

KEY:

Breast pain	— BP	Headache	— HD	Fighting	— FT
Bloatedness	— BLT	Depression	— DP	Cramps	— CMP
Crying	— CRY	Anxiety	— ANX	Period	— P

Do You Have Premenstrual Syndrome?

PMS MENSTRUAL CALENDAR
MONTH February

Sunday	Monday	Tuesday	Wednesday	Thursday	Friday	Saturday
	1	2	3	4	5	6 DP BP
7 BP DP CRY	8 BP DP CRY	9 BP BLT ANX	10 HD BP BLT ANX	11 CMP BP BLT ANX	12 HD CMP BP Thirst	13 HD Thirst BP CRY
14 P	15 P	16 P	17 P	18	19	20
21	22	23	24	25	26	27
28						

KEY:

Breast pain	— BP	Headache	— HD	Fighting	— FT
Bloatedness	— BLT	Depression	— DP	Cramps	— CMP
Crying	— CRY	Anxiety	— ANX	Period	— P

43

PMS MENSTRUAL CALENDAR
MONTH _March_

Sunday	Monday	Tuesday	Wednesday	Thursday	Friday	Saturday
	1	2	3	4	5 BP FT CRY	6 BP BLT CRY
7 HD CMP BP CRY	8 HD CMP BP BLT	9 HD Thirst BP CRY	10 BP BLT FT CRY	11 P	12 P	13 P
14 P	15 P	16	17	18	19	20
21	22	23	24	25	26	27
28	29	30	31			

KEY:

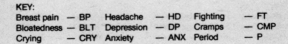

Breast pain — BP	Headache — HD	Fighting — FT	
Bloatedness — BLT	Depression — DP	Cramps — CMP	
Crying — CRY	Anxiety — ANX	Period — P	

Do You Have Premenstrual Syndrome?

PMS MENSTRUAL CALENDAR
MONTH _April_

Sunday	Monday	Tuesday	Wednesday	Thursday	Friday	Saturday
				1	2	3
4 HD ANX	5 ANX FT	6 HD CRY FT	7 CMP BP BLT	8 HD Thirst BP	9 P	10 P
11 P	12 P	13 P	14	15	16	17
18	19	20	21	22	23	24
25	26	27	28	29	30	

KEY:
Breast pain — BP   Headache — HD   Fighting — FT
Bloatedness — BLT   Depression — DP   Cramps — CMP
Crying — CRY   Anxiety — ANX   Period — P

When It's Not PMS

Keeping a chart can indicate if your symptoms are connected to your menstrual period, and can also tell you if the symptoms may be due to another cause.

Marsha, 34, is an editor of a well-known fashion magazine. She had many symptoms, such as headaches, anxiety, irritability, hostility, nausea, and diarrhea, which recurred about once a month. Furthermore, after the birth of her first child a year ago, the symptoms suddenly became much worse. Marsha wondered if she had PMS. She asked her gynecologist about it. After giving her a thorough medical exam, which revealed nothing physically wrong, her doctor suggested she keep a monthly chart of her symptoms. The results were surprising.

Marsha could plainly see that her symptoms did not coincide with her menstrual period. What, then, was the cause for the headaches, the anxiety, the diarrhea?

She realized that her symptoms regularly occurred during the week before her monthly magazine deadline, which was around the fifteenth of every month. Marsha was under a tremendous amount of pressure during this time. The extreme stress of her job was expressed physically as headaches, nausea, and diarrhea. The anxiety she felt each time the deadline approached resulted in irritability and hostility toward others. Her symptoms became worse after the birth of her daughter because the responsibility of caring for a baby placed extra demands on her time and on her emotions. Furthermore, being a working mother caused her to feel some conflict and guilt, especially during those days when the impending deadline forced her to work extra hours.

Premenstrual tension was not the cause of Marsha's symptoms, yet by charting her bodily and emotional feelings she gained some important self-knowledge. Marsha is now reducing her work load during the week of the deadline and is also seeing a counselor on a short-term basis to sort out some of her unresolved feelings about motherhood and her career ambitions.

As you can see, the symptoms alone do not constitute a diagnosis

Do You Have Premenstrual Syndrome?

PMS MENSTRUAL CALENDAR

MONTH _July_

Sunday	Monday	Tuesday	Wednesday	Thursday	Friday	Saturday
				1	2	3
4	5	6	7	8	9	10 ANX
11 ANX	12 HD ANX IRT	13 HD HST NS	14 HD ANX IRT	15 ANX HD HST IRT	16	17
18	19	20	21	22	23	24
25	26	27 P	28 P	29 P	30 P	31 P

KEY:

Headache	— HD	Hostility	— HST	Cramps	— CMP
Anxiety	— ANX	Nausea	— NS	Period	— P
Irritability	— IRT	Diarrhea	— DRH		

PMS MENSTRUAL CALENDAR
MONTH August

Sunday	Monday	Tuesday	Wednesday	Thursday	Friday	Saturday
1	2	3	4	5	6	7
8	9 HD ANX HST	10 HD IRT NS	11 HD NS DRH	12 ANX HD IRT NS	13 NS DRH HD IRT	14
15	16	17	18	19	20	21
22	23	24	25	26 P CMP	27 P	28 P
29 P	30	31				

KEY:

Headache	— HD	Hostility	— HST	Cramps	— CMP
Anxiety	— ANX	Nausea	— NS	Period	— P
Irritability	— IRT	Diarrhea	— DRH		

Do You Have Premenstrual Syndrome?

PMS MENSTRUAL CALENDAR
MONTH September

Sunday	Monday	Tuesday	Wednesday	Thursday	Friday	Saturday
			1	2	3	4
5	6	7	8 ANX	9 ANX	10 HD ANX	11 HD
12 HD	13 HST IRT NS	14 ANX HST NS DRH	15 ANX HST NS DRH	16	17	18
19	20	21	22 P CMP	23 P CMP	24 P	25 P
26	27	28	29	30		

KEY:

Headache	— HD	Hostility	— HST	Cramps	— CMP
Anxiety	— ANX	Nausea	— NS	Period	— P
Irritability	— IRT	Diarrhea	— DRH		

49

PMS MENSTRUAL CALENDAR
MONTH *October*

Sunday	Monday	Tuesday	Wednesday	Thursday	Friday	Saturday
					1	2
3	4	5	6	7	8	9
10	11 HD ANX	12 HD IRT ANX	13 HD NS DRH IRT	14 NS DRH HD IRT	15 NS DRH HD HST	16
17	18	19 P CMP	20 P	21 P	22 P	23 P
24	25	26	27	28	29	30

KEY:
Headache — HD Hostility — HST Cramps — CMP
Anxiety — ANX Nausea — NS Period — P
Irritability — IRT Diarrhea — DRH

of premenstrual syndrome. As mentioned before, it does not matter so much *what* the symptoms are, as *when* they occur.

Keeping Your Own Chart

Keeping a record of when the symptoms occur is probably the most important diagnostic method currently available to determine whether a woman has premenstrual syndrome.

This book provides you with a six-month chart that you can fill out. Most doctors agree that the symptoms as well as the menstrual cycle should be recorded for at least three months before a diagnosis of premenstrual syndrome can be made. Some physicians advise keeping a record for six months since it can take that long to establish a clear pattern.

Using the charts in this book, first fill out the appropriate month. Then mark in the dates. When you experience a symptom or symptoms, write them down on the day they occur. Continue to include each symptom every day you experience it. In addition, mark the first day of your period and each day there is menstrual bleeding. Some women use abbreviations or symbols to simplify their chart keeping. Others prefer to write them out. In addition, it may be helpful to incorporate the degree of intensity you feel for each symptom. For example, a "1" can indicate mild pain, "2" moderate pain, and "3" severe pain. Write the number next to the symptom. You might also want to mark any external events that take place such as deadlines, accidents, family illness, or a stressful situation at home or on the job.

Beyond the diagnostic use for PMS, one of the best reasons for keeping a chart is to learn more about your unique rhythms and cycles, both physical and emotional. This self-knowledge can be invaluable as you learn to cope with premenstrual syndrome or if you decide to seek professional health care.

You can also use the chart to track improvements as you try the various treatments suggested in this book. Seeing the results can increase your sense of control.

PMS MENSTRUAL CALENDAR

MONTH_____

Sunday	Monday	Tuesday	Wednesday	Thursday	Friday	Saturday

Suggested symptom key code shown on earlier charts.

Additional notes:_____

_____

_____

Do You Have Premenstrual Syndrome?

PMS MENSTRUAL CALENDAR
MONTH_____

Sunday	Monday	Tuesday	Wednesday	Thursday	Friday	Saturday

Suggested symptom key code shown on earlier charts.

Additional notes:_____

_____

_____

PMS MENSTRUAL CALENDAR
MONTH_____

Sunday	Monday	Tuesday	Wednesday	Thursday	Friday	Saturday

Suggested symptom key code shown on earlier charts.

Additional notes:_____
_____
_____

Do You Have Premenstrual Syndrome?

PMS MENSTRUAL CALENDAR
MONTH_____

Sunday	Monday	Tuesday	Wednesday	Thursday	Friday	Saturday

Suggested symptom key code shown on earlier charts.

Additional notes:_____

_____

_____

PMS MENSTRUAL CALENDAR
MONTH_____

Sunday	Monday	Tuesday	Wednesday	Thursday	Friday	Saturday

Suggested symptom key code shown on earlier charts.

Additional notes:_____

_____

_____

Do You Have Premenstrual Syndrome?

PMS MENSTRUAL CALENDAR

MONTH_____

Sunday	Monday	Tuesday	Wednesday	Thursday	Friday	Saturday

Suggested symptom key code shown on earlier charts.

Additional notes:_____

_____

_____

If You Have PMS

If, after you keep a record for several months, a pattern emerges that indicates your particular set of symptoms occurs during the several days before your menstrual period, you most likely have premenstrual syndrome.

Knowing you have PMS and being able to predict when your symptoms will occur can help you to cope with them better. Just being able to say, "I know why I'm feeling so sad. I know why I'm irritable. I know why I've put on three pounds. I know why my breasts hurt," can help immeasurably. The fear of the unknown is removed once you understand that premenstrual syndrome is the cause of your symptoms.

Should You See a Doctor?

You feel fairly certain you have premenstrual syndrome. The symptoms recur monthly several days before the onset of your period and disappear once your menstrual flow starts. Is it necessary to receive medical care? Should you see a doctor?

First, let us say that the majority of women who have PMS can find ways to relieve the discomfort and pain by themselves. Experience has shown that self-help methods are extremely effective in alleviating most PMS symptoms. Chapters 8 and 10 in this book will show how women have learned to overcome their symptoms through diet, exercise, and over-the-counter medications, as well as through changes in life style. Chances are good you can find relief through these methods, too.

Most doctors and other health-care specialists suggest trying self-help treatments first. If, however, there is no measurable improvement in a woman's condition, they then recommend she consult a doctor. Use the chart in this chapter to help your doctor pinpoint your condition.

In any case, a woman should be aware that many of the physical manifestations of PMS can and should be treated symptomatically. For example, recurrent cystitis is usually caused by bacterial infection and should be treated appropriately, even if it occurs only during the premenstruum. There is no reason why a woman should suffer from a physical symptom just because it happens right before the start of her period.

Furthermore, psychological symptoms may exist throughout the cycle but get worse during the premenstruum and may, therefore, be noticed only at that time. The underlying psychological problem has to be resolved before there can be any relief of the PMS-intensified (but not PMS-caused) symptoms. This can be achieved through psychotherapy, counseling, and/or appropriate prescription medication.

Finally, you should be aware of certain symptoms that may be related to the reproductive organs or to the menstrual cycle but are not associated with PMS. They may be indicative of another disease or disorder and therefore should be brought to the attention of a doctor. If you are experiencing any of the following symptoms, contact a physician right away.

- Excessive bleeding during menstruation (saturating two sanitary napkins in one hour).
- Bleeding or spotting during times other than during your menstrual period.
- Excessively long menstrual periods (lasting over ten days) or continual bleeding from the vagina.
- Abnormal menstrual periods (unusual bleeding pattern or great pain either before or during menstruation).
- Absence of menstrual period or unusually scant flow.
- Pain with intercourse (before, during, or after menstruation).
- Extreme continuous depression whether or not it can be related to the menstrual cycle.
- Severe continuous headaches or migraines that are not relieved by conventional pain-relief medication.
- Visual blurring, spots in front of the eyes, tunnel vision, whether or not it is related to menstruation.
- Lumps or fibers in the breast that do not disappear once menstruation starts.

- Vomiting or severe diarrhea that lasts for more than several days, regardless of the menstrual cycle.
- Any symptom accompanied by severe pain or fever.

Any of the above symptoms warrants immediate medical attention.

In conclusion, most women who have the symptoms of PMS are able to identify their own condition correctly and can find relief through self-help methods.

Between 2.5 percent and 5 percent of women experience premenstrual syndrome in its most severe form and need appropriate and compassionate treatment from the medical community. If your symptoms are overwhelming you, if you cannot alleviate your pain by diet or drugstore medications, you may want to contact a doctor.

Because not every doctor is familiar with the problems associated with PMS and can give you the help you need, you may have to do some searching before finding the appropriate medical care. Chapter 10 of this book will suggest ways to find a doctor who is right for you.

If your symptoms are severe, it may be advisable to have a complete and thorough general and gynecological examination in order to rule out any physical disorder that might actually be causing the symptoms. The chart of your monthly symptoms may help your doctor make an accurate diagnosis should you develop certain gynecological problems.

Whether her symptoms are mild, moderate, or severe, almost every woman who has PMS reports that one of the greatest moments of relief came when she knew her symptoms had a name and that she was not the only one to feel this way. If you suffer from PMS, you probably feel the same way. You're not alone and you're not going crazy. PMS is very real and is shared by millions of women. It is not a sign of inherent instability, nor does it mean that you lack will power or self-control.

In fact, most women who suffer from menstrual-related distress show a remarkable degree of courage, endurance, and fortitude in the face of pain. This is an inner strength many women do not even realize they have.

By recognizing these qualities in yourself, you can begin to play an important role in your own health care. You've already achieved the first step—you know what PMS is and whether you have it. Now you can learn how to find the means and the methods to conquer premenstrual syndrome.

3

WHY PREMENSTRUAL SYNDROME OCCURS

Your Monthly Cycle

It's fascinating to learn about your own body and how it works. I have found that I can cope a little better with PMS now that I know what's going on. In any case, I can at least understand what my doctor is telling me.

Katie G., 28
Real-estate agent

The Puzzle of PMS

Many theories have been advanced as to why premenstrual syndrome occurs. Some believe PMS can be pinpointed to a hormonal deficiency. Others claim it is caused by hormonal imbalance. Still others are studying the possibility of vitamin deficiencies, periodic hypoglycemia (low blood sugar), water retention, neuroendocrine changes, abnormality in hormone absorption or excretion, allergic reactions to certain hormones, as well as excess production of various different hormones. Furthermore, many psychological and cultural influences are thought to play a powerful role in the physical experience of PMS. It seems there are almost as many theories about the cause of PMS as there are symptoms.

Some researchers question the quest for one sure-fire solution to PMS. It may be that no answer has yet been found because researchers are looking for a simple answer to a very complex problem.

Although some doctors and researchers believe they have found *the* cause and *the* cure for premenstrual symptoms, in reality none of these theories have been proven in rigorously controlled scientific clinical studies. Even though many PMS sufferers have found some symptomatic relief, too many pieces are still missing in the PMS puzzle.

Whatever the ultimate solution may turn out to be, the woman seeking relief from PMS today faces a baffling array of advice, counseling, and treatments that can result in a frustrating and expensive search for a safe medical cure that may not yet exist.

Lindsay Leckie, founder of the National PMS Society in Durham, North Carolina, encourages women to be "their own healthcare advocates" when it comes to PMS. As long as the puzzle remains incomplete, we must do what we can to find out just what is known and what the possible causes and solutions may be.

Therefore, in order to begin to understand the nature of PMS, it is vital to learn about the inner workings of your own body, particularly your menstrual cycle.

Knowing how the process of menstruation works can help you identify what is normal and what is not and can give you the real information you need to help ease some of the symptoms of PMS. This knowledge can also be of value should you decide to talk to a doctor or gynecologist about your monthly symptoms.

The Menstrual Cycle

The word "menstruation" is derived from the Latin word "menses," meaning "months." The process of menstruation is sometimes described medically as the menses. We talk about the monthly cycle or "that time of the month."

The menstrual cycle may occur once a month for some women, but it can span anywhere from 20 to 45 days and still be considered normal. There is also a good deal of variation within the menstrual cycles of individual women over the months and years. Very few women are completely regular in their cycles over an extended period of time. The statistical average places menstruation every 28 days, but only 16 percent of women actually have 28-day cycles.

Hormones are chemical substances formed in special glands such as the pituitary. The hormones then travel via the bloodstream to their specific target organs, activating the various physical processes—for example, the menstrual cycle.

The most familiar "female" hormones are estrogen and progesterone. They are primarily produced by the ovaries.

Estrogen promotes the development and maintenance of the reproductive organs (ovaries, fallopian tubes, uterus, vagina, vulva, and clitoris) as well as the secondary female sexual characteristics (breasts, nipples, pubic hair, higher pitched voice, and soft skin due to deposition of body fat). In the menstrual cycle, estrogen is essential to the maturation of the eggs, or ova. Some believe that too much estrogen in the post-ovulatory phase causes the symptoms of PMS.

The primary function of *progesterone* is to thicken the uterine lining and ready the various support systems to maintain a pregnancy. A good amount of speculation about PMS has centered around this hormone, since it is present only in the second half of the cycle and only if ovulation has occurred. Some think that too little progesterone results in PMS. Others feel that an imbalance in the ratio of progesterone to estrogen is the source of PMS.

There are three other important but less well-known hormones involved in the menstrual cycle. These hormones—the *follicle stimulating hormone* (FSH), the *luteinizing hormone* (LH), and the *luteotropic hormone* (LTH)—are secreted by the pituitary, and they work together to control the ovaries. Without these hormones, the ovaries could not properly produce estrogen and progesterone.

It is known that a problem with the hypothalamus, the pituitary, or any of these five major reproductive hormones can interfere with the normal process of the menstrual cycle. One reason why no simple answer has yet been found to PMS may be that in different women PMS stems from different hormonal disorders.

What Happens During the Menstrual Cycle

The female body has two ovaries attached by ligaments to the outside wall of the uterus. Shortly after the onset of menstrual flow, estrogen production increases. As it does, one ovary starts to prepare an egg, or ovum. The maturing ovum is encased in a minute sac, called the *Graafian follicle.* This follicle swells, growing up to 1.5 centimeters in diameter (about a half inch) as it prepares for ovulation.

Meanwhile, as soon as menstrual flow stops, the uterus begins building up a lining called the *endometrium*, rich in blood, and special glands to support a fertilized egg. All this takes place in the first half of the menstrual cycle. This part of the menstrual pattern goes by several names, including the pre-ovulatory phase, the follicular phase, or the proliferative phase.

At the moment of ovulation, the swollen Graafian follicle ruptures, releasing the mature egg. This marks the start of the second half of the menstrual cycle. It is known as the post-ovulatory phase, the luteal phase, the secretory phase, or the premenstrual phase.

Immediately after ovulation, the egg enters the Fallopian tube, which is connected to the interior of the uterus. As the egg travels through the tube, it can be fertilized by sperm. In a short amount of time, the empty Graafian follicle is transformed into what is called the *corpus luteum* (yellow body). The corpus luteum then begins

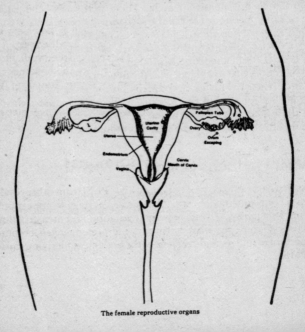

The female reproductive organs

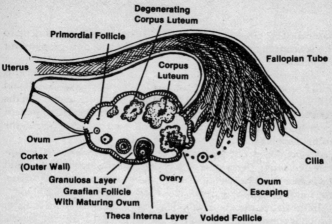

The ovarian cycle, starting with the primordial follicle, the growth of the Graafian follicle containing the maturing ovum (egg), the moment of ovulation with the ovum escaping, the development of the corpus luteum and its degeneration

to manufacture and secrete progesterone, which is necessary to build up the uterine lining in preparation for a fertilized egg.

When conception does not occur, the corpus luteum disintegrates and progesterone levels drop. This causes the endometrial lining to break down, and it is shed from the uterus, initiating the familiar menstrual flow.

The cycle then repeats itself. In this manner, a fresh new uterine lining is formed once per cycle.

The Timing of Hormones

As described earlier, what distinguishes PMS from other conditions is the element of *timing*. The symptoms seem to appear only during that period of time between ovulation and menstruation. Therefore, knowing what hormones are present *when* becomes important to understanding some of the possible underlying causes of PMS.

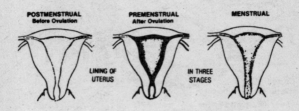

The uterine cycle

The reproductive hormones are not constantly present throughout the menstrual cycle. Instead, they increase and diminish, each hormone following its own rhythm, controlled by various feedback mechanisms.

The following graph can help you visualize the cyclical fluctuation of hormones.

Ovulation and PMS

The first half of the cycle is usually a symptom-free time for most PMS sufferers. The problems begin around the time of ovulation. The discomfort and pain can start at any point between ovulation and menstruation.

Therefore, if you have, or think you have, PMS, it becomes important to be able to tell when ovulation takes place. This information will also be needed by most doctors and clinics involved in treating PMS.

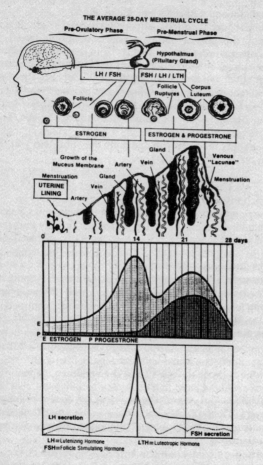

The ovarian follicle, the uterine lining, and the major reproductive hormones over the course of one 28-day menstrual
cycle

How can a woman know when she ovulates?

One simple way is to look at your menstrual chart. It is now known that the post-ovulatory phase lasts almost exactly two weeks. In other words, it takes 14 days from the moment of ovulation to the onset of menstruation. The pre-ovulatory phase can vary greatly in time, but once ovulation takes place, if there is no pregnancy, menstruation invariably begins two weeks later. Therefore, to determine when you ovulated, note the date on your chart when your period began and count backward two weeks. That is the day you most likely ovulated.

Other changes take place in the body that can help you detect ovulation on the day it occurs.

Ovarian Changes

Some women notice an ache or a pain in their lower abdomen sometime between their menstrual periods. It usually lasts several hours and sometimes as long as several days. This phenomenon is often called "mittelschmerz," a German word referring to the discomfort accompanying ovulation.

Not all women experience mittelschmerz every month even though ovulation may take place quite normally. Women on the Pill will not feel this mid-cycle discomfort since oral contraceptives suppress ovulation.

What does mittelschmerz feel like? The sensation has been described by some as an abdominal cramp. Others notice a dull ache. Still others experience a distinctly sharp pain. Mittelschmerz is felt either on the right or the left side of the abdomen, depending on which ovary had ovulated that cycle. For some reason, this sensation seems to become more noticeable with age. It may be that some women gradually become more attuned to their bodily signals.

Although most women who experience mittelschmerz report that the feeling is uncomfortable but tolerable, some women endure extremely severe pain. In this case, mittelschmerz can be easily misdiagnosed as a pelvic infection or even appendicitis, especially if the pain is on the lower right side of the abdomen. Usually, appendicitis is accompanied by fever, nausea and vomiting; however, if there is any doubt about any acute pain, a doctor should be contacted immediately.

The pain of ovulation may be due to several causes.

One might be the dramatic growth of the Graafian follicle. A day or so before ovulation, it swells enormously and may occupy as much as one-fourth of the ovary. This can cause sensitivity or soreness in the abdominal region.

Another possible cause is the rupture of the Graafian follicle. This moment of ovulation, in some women, produces the pain of mittelschmerz.

A third reason may be intra-abdominal bleeding at the site of the erupted Graafian follicle.

Finally, it is postulated that an increased amount of prostaglandins (a hormone-like substance) produced during ovulation may account for the pain.

Occasionally, ovulation is attended by a little blood-tinged discharge from the vagina, called "spotting" or "breakthrough bleeding." Spotting is probably due to spillage of estrogen when the Graafian follicle ruptures. The hormone can cause uterine contractions and the shedding of some of the endometrial lining, resulting in vaginal bleeding.

Should you notice any short-lived abdominal ache or pain sometime during the middle of your cycle, mark this on your menstrual chart. If two weeks later your period starts, then this was probably a sign of ovulation.

Temperature Changes

Another way to determine when ovulation takes place is to measure basal body temperature (BBT), or the temperature the body registers when at rest. This method may be familiar to those who practice natural birth control.

The temperature method is based on the way estrogen and progesterone affect basal body temperature. Estrogen tends to depress BBT while progesterone raises it. This fluctuation is very slight, only a few fractions of a degree.

During the pre-ovulatory phase of the cycle, only estrogen is

TEMPERATURE CHART

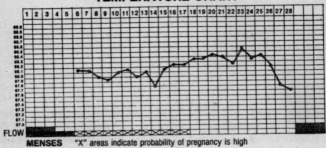

MENSES   "X" areas indicate probability of pregnancy is high

Basal body temperature over the course of one 28-day menstrual cycle

present and temperature readings will be relatively on the low side. On the day of ovulation, the temperature usually dips a small but noticeable percentage of a degree. As soon as progesterone begins to be produced, BBT rises about one degree. Temperature continues to increase slightly until a day or so before menstruation begins. A persistently high BBT usually is one of the first signs that conception has occurred.

Normal cyclical basal body temperature can be affected by a low-grade infection or a fever, however slight.

Only about 25 percent of all women show a discernible difference in BBT between the pre-ovulatory and post-ovulatory phases. Furthermore, a study recently performed at the Masters and Johnson Institute in St. Louis has found that this shift in temperature may not be as closely linked to the day of ovulation as was previously believed.

However, for some, this method may provide a clue to when ovulation has occurred. In any case, some doctors who treat women who suffer from PMS request that a daily BBT record be kept along with the chart for symptoms. Your doctor or pharmacist can instruct you in the proper way to measure your BBT.

Cervical Changes

Yet another method to determine the day of ovulation is to note the changes in the cervical discharge that collects in the vagina. This method has recently begun to be used as a means of natural birth control.

The cervix has special mucous glands that are affected by the ebb and flow of hormones. The first few days after menstrual flow has stopped, little or no mucus is produced by the cervix. These are called "dry" days. As estrogen levels begin to increase, cervical mucus appears at the vaginal opening. The mucus is thick, sticky, and opaque (usually white or yellow). It covers the opening of the uterus, preventing harmful bacteria from entering. The thickness of the mucus also lowers sperm motility.

As soon as LH secretion starts, the cervical mucus begins to

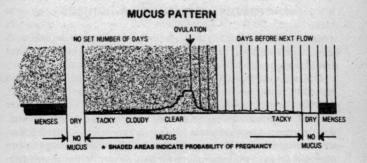

MUCUS PATTERN

Cervical mucus as it appears at the vulva over the course of one 28-day menstrual cycle

change. It becomes clear and slippery, resembling the texture of raw egg white. The amount of cervical mucus increases considerably just prior to ovulation. These are referred to as "wet" days. This change encourages a most favorable environment for sperm movement and survival.

About three or four days after ovulation, in the presence of progesterone and estrogen, the cervical mucus goes through another change. It once again becomes thick and opaque, inhibiting sperm motility. Once the hormone levels fall, the amount of cervical mucus is reduced and there is usually another period of "dry" days shortly before menstruation begins.

The natural mucus pattern can be altered by the use of spermicides, douching, vaginitis, or if surgery has been performed on the cervix.

Your doctor or gynecologist can provide further information about this method of determining ovulation. In addition, being familiar with your normal cervical discharges can help you spot anything unusual that may indicate an infection or other diseases in an early stage.

Premenstrual Uterine Changes

Many women with PMS report feeling cramping during the days before menstruation. It is not completely understood why this should happen, although some theories have been offered. One holds that an abnormally low amount of progesterone permits the cramping to occur. Another theory suggests that excess prostaglandins produce the premenstrual uterine spasms.

It is possible for doctors and trained observers to determine what point in the menstrual cycle a woman is in by performing an endometrial biopsy. This examination is done in some cases of infertility and as a means to check for uterine cancer. But it can also be performed for reasons related to PMS. A few studies of women who committed violent crime and suicide attempts have included endometrial biopsy information to determine when those acts occurred in relation to the menstrual cycle. The endometrial biopsy cannot, however, be used to diagnose PMS.

Premenstrual Vaginal Changes

Along with cyclical changes in the cervix and uterus, the vagina is also affected by estrogen and progesterone.

As estrogen increases, so does the thickness of the vaginal walls. This allows the top layer of cells to peel off, permitting new cell layers to form. In this way, the vagina is constantly renewing itself. During the pre-ovulatory phase, vaginal secretions are acid, preventing the growth of harmful bacteria.

After ovulation, when estrogen is dropping, the vagina loses its acidity. This may be one reason why vaginal infections often take place in the week or so before menstruation. Vaginitis is an unpleasant, yet treatable, symptom of PMS. Again, by being aware of your normal vaginal discharge, you are in a better position to detect possible infections or other abnormalities early.

Some women experience vaginal dryness toward the end of the cycle, often making intercourse uncomfortable or painful. This may, in part, account for a decrease in sexual desire during PMS time. Appropriate sexual stimulation can increase a woman's level of arousal whereby the vagina produces natural lubrication.

On the other hand, some women feel at their sexual peak right before the start of their period. This might be due to the retention of bodily fluids in many organs, including the uterus, breasts, and vagina. This congestion puts pressure on the sexual organs, increasing sexual sensation and arousal.

Premenstrual Changes of the Clitoris

During the luteal phase, many women retain fluids. The swelling that may result extends to the sexual organs, including the vagina, the vulva, and the clitoris. The pressure on the clitoris may feel similar to the engorgement during heightened sexual arousal.

For some women, this pressure produces greater desire for sex and orgasm. Occasionally, though, the pressure can cause the clitoris to become extremely sensitive. Direct stimulation or vigorous sexual intercourse may then produce pain instead of pleasure.

The drop in hormone levels after the onset of menstruation makes the swelling disappear.

Premenstrual Changes of the Breasts

In the post-ovulatory phase, the combined effect of estrogen and progesterone often causes the breasts to feel swollen and more sensitive. Some women particularly enjoy sexual stimulation of the breasts at this time. For some, however, the breasts become so sensitive as to be painful.

Occasionally, the pain is so intense just before menstruation that a woman can barely put on a bra or wear close clothing on the breasts.

Often, a woman will notice lumps or cysts in one or both breasts. They may feel granular or fibrous. Any kind of change like this can scare a woman terribly. Usually, these cysts or fibers disappear once menstruation begins.

Most doctors feel that water retention causes the tenderness along with the cystic formations. Later on, we'll discuss some recommended self-treatments (such as avoiding caffeine and taking diuretics) that have helped many overcome this PMS symptom. We'll also take a look at various medical treatments.

Since breast self-examination is an important part of a woman's health care, she should know that the most reliable time to perform this exam is one week after the start of the menstrual flow.

Any breast changes that do not disappear shortly after menstruation should be brought to a physician's attention at once.

Other Premenstrual Changes

In this chapter, we have focused on the effects of the sexual hormones on the reproductive organs. Of course, PMS often involves many different parts of the body. In Chapter 5 we'll examine some of the physical symptoms more closely.

Psychological changes are certainly associated with the premenstrual phase, although no one knows why one woman may feel "bitchy as hell," another like "crying a river," and still another like "conquering the world." This is a particularly complex and controversial aspect of any discussion about PMS and we'll explore it more fully in Chapter 6.

The menstrual cycle is a normal and healthy cyclical pattern. The elegant interplay of hormones and their precision timing is a dazzling example of the beauty of the human body. By understanding the intricate steps of the cycle, a woman can gain greater appreciation of herself and her body.

The female hormonal pattern is not as delicate or fragile as is commonly believed. It has amazing recuperative abilities even when put through stress, illness, personal tragedy, extreme dieting, excessive exercise, and other circumstances that can temporarily interrupt a normal pattern.

Yet it is well known that an event such as childbirth can throw the cycle off its normal course for quite some time. Many women with PMS recall that it was only after giving birth that the symptoms turned severe. Oral contraceptives, abortion, hormone treatments, and gynecological surgery can also dramatically affect the normal hormonal balance and timing. Sometimes, with care and time, the cycle can realign itself. Sometimes, however, it does not.

4

PREMENSTRUAL SYNDROME AND YOUR MENSTRUAL PERIOD

For about five to seven days before my period, my breasts ache, my head feels as if it's in a vise, I am depressed and tense. Then my period starts. Just as all those other symptoms clear up, I am hit with paralyzing cramps. Pain like hot irons inside. It's awful. For me, it's a double whammy.

Debra F., 29
Grade-school teacher

PMS and Your Period

Menstruation and PMS are inexorably linked. Without the menstrual cycle, a woman would not experience the premenstrual symptoms. Therefore, no careful examination of the causes and cures of PMS would be complete without considering the physical, psychological, and social aspects of menstruation.

In part, premenstrual and menstrual pain can be linked to society's overall negative attitude toward the entire menstrual process. These attitudes are integrated into a woman's psyche and influence her self-perception. How different the premenstrual time would be if the event of menstruation were greeted with champagne and praise instead of shame and secrecy.

In no way does this mean, however that the pain is emotional or "all in your head." PMS and menstrual pain have physical causes, some of which have only recently been discovered. How that pain, or any pain, is handled does very much depend on personality and societal influences. Learning about those influences may help you gain a better understanding of your own condition.

Although many women who suffer from premenstrual syndrome find relief once their period begins, other women say PMS is just a prelude to their menstrual cramps. So, if you suffer from PMS and from menstrual pain, this chapter is for you. In addition to talking about some of the social and personal influences of menstruation, you will learn how to alleviate some, if not most, of your menstrual pain. A more comfortable period may, in turn, reduce some of the symptoms associated with PMS.

So, to begin, let's start by answering the questions most women ask about menstruation: What is normal, and why is it so painful?

What Is Normal?

Probably the most important factor to remember when talking about menstruation and normality is that there are no absolutes. The pattern for menstrual cycles over a lifetime seems to be as characteristic as fingerprints. Each individual woman experiences, in her own unique way, her menstrual cycles that change continually from puberty to menopause.

As we have seen in the previous chapter, the length of the cycle can vary enormously and still be normal. The duration and amount of menstrual flow can change considerably and be regarded as normal. Menstrual periods can vary from month to month and year to year. Premenstrual symptoms can change, too. It seems that as a woman grows older, the number of symptoms and their intensity increase; but each month can bring a variation.

Surprisingly little solid statistical work has been done on the range of normality in the area of menstruation. More knowledge has been gathered about what color dish detergent women prefer to buy than about the way women experience their menstrual cycles over a lifetime.

What we do know is most women do not have the "statistical average" 28-day cycle year after year. Your own calendar may tell you that the length of your cycles varies frequently. In fact, only a small percentage of women have regular cycles that vary less than six days over a year's time.

Teenagers and women in their early twenties have enormous variation from cycle to cycle. It appears that the cycles become most stable in women who are between the ages of 25 and 39 (even though there is still some variability). After forty, the cycles gradually become more irregular until menopause, when menstruation ceases.

The duration of menstrual flow also varies from woman to woman and from cycle to cycle. Bleeding that lasts between three and seven days is physiologically normal. However, periods that are only one or two days long or that last over a week may be indicative of a possible physical disorder. If this is the case with you, you may want to consult your doctor. And if there is an abrupt change in the duration of your menstrual bleeding, or if your periods seem to be lasting longer and getting more painful, it would be wise to see your gynecologist. But if your periods are usually eight or nine days long and are not accompanied by other symptoms, relax. Chances are you are perfectly normal.

You might also wonder whether the amount of menstrual flow you experience each cycle is normal. Well, like the length of the cycle and the duration of the flow, the amount of blood shed during each menstrual period also varies. If some of your cycles are accompanied by a heavier or scantier flow than others, this, too, is perfectly normal.

Gynecologists report that the average amount of blood shed during menstruation is about two ounces, but anything between one and six ounces is considered to fall within the normal range. Again, if there is an abrupt change in the amount of menstrual flow, if its color does not seem normal, or if there is excessive bleeding, especially if accompanied by extreme pain or fever, contact your physician immediately.

Most women experience the heaviest flow on the first or second day of menstruation. As the days progress, the flow lessens until it has stopped. This is the normal progress of the menstrual period.

Sometimes, though, a woman might experience spotting or light bleeding for several days before her period. Then cramps and heavy bleeding begin and she knows her period has actually started. This symptom might be mistaken for part of premenstrual syndrome but it may be indicative of a more serious disorder. Check with your doctor.

It is important to understand that normal menstrual bleeding itself is not unhealthy and does not mean something is wrong. Actually the word "bleeding" is something of a misnomer since menstrual "blood" is not the same blood as is circulating through the arteries and veins and the "bleeding" is not caused by an injury or a wound. In fact, menstrual blood differs essentially from the other blood in the body in that it doesn't clot.

What if you notice occasional clots in your menstrual flow—is that normal? Usually, it is. Sometimes bits of cervical mucus are surrounded by menstrual blood, which then resemble clots.

Other times, though, clots are formed when cramps or uterine contractions cause tiny blood vessels in the uterus to rupture when the lining is sloughed off. In this case, a tiny amount of real blood (which clots) is lost along with the menstrual flow.

As long as the clots are small, they are normal and common in most menstruating women. Clots that are larger than a half-dollar may signal physical abnormality and should be reported to your doctor.

As you can see, there is tremendous variability in the menstrual process. Unless there is a physiological disorder, no woman need think of herself as irregular or abnormal because her menstrual patterns do not match some mythical average.

The same can be said for premenstrual syndrome. Quite a few women feel uncertain or anxious when they realize their bodies are changing—especially when the changes can be related to the menstrual cycle. Like many women, you may have wondered whether you are becoming neurotic or imagining things. But be assured that premenstrual symptoms are real and have physiological causes, as do menstrual pain and cramping.

What Causes the Pain?

Almost all women experience some cramping or discomfort during the first day or so of menstruation. Pain is usually a normal part of menstruation, both premenstrually and during the days of flow. In fact, it can be said that menstruation and childbirth are the only natural, healthy functions of human beings that are normally accompanied by pain.

The pain often begins several days before menstruation starts. Many women notice slight cramping in the lower abdomen that seems to increase in intensity until the day just prior to menstruation. For some, the start of the flow brings marked relief. For others, the first day of menstruation is the most painful. After a day or so, the pain decreases in intensity.

The amount of pain can vary among women. Furthermore, individuals have different tolerance levels for pain. For some women, menstrual cramps are mild. For others they are moderately painful and for still others the pain can be severe.

Anyone who has experienced severe menstrual cramps (spasmodic dysmenorrhea) would recognize the most common symptoms—a burning, sharp pain in the lower abdomen, pain that radiates out to the genitals, buttocks, and inside of upper thighs, legs that feel leaden, a general feeling of weakness, nausea, vomiting, diarrhea, and/or dizziness.

Many women have been alarmed at the intensity of their pain. Indeed, it can be so severe, especially during its onset, that a woman may be in a near state of shock or near blacking out from the pain.

Of the 75 million women in America of childbearing age, approximately 5 percent or 3.5 million women are almost completely incapacitated for 24 to 48 hours each month by menstrual distress.

In the past, this pain was thought to be imaginary or "all in a woman's head." Many men and women themselves chastised those who became bedridden once a month. It was felt that menstruation was being used as an excuse to be self-indulgent, bad tempered, or to get out of unpleasant activities.

Granted a few women might use menstruation to manipulate others, but most women who have dysmenorrhea are in too much physical pain to think of anything but surviving those severe spasms and somehow getting through the day.

Scientists and physicians now understand more about the physiology of the uterus and the process of menstruating.

For example, it is now believed that painful periods are related to ovulation. For reasons not yet completely understood, in cycles that are not accompanied by ovulation (anovulatory cycles) there is often reduced or no menstrual pain. This is supported by the fact that women who take birth-control pills, which suppress ovulation, experience very little cramping. In addition, the first year or so of menstrual cycles are anovulatory in many girls, which explains why cramping does not usually begin until an adolescent is somewhat older. Even in adult women, one or two cycles per year may be anovulatory. Periods that follow may be blessedly mild.

More is now known about the strength of the uterine muscle. It is the strongest muscle in the human body—stronger than the heart and more powerful than the most developed biceps of a weight lifter. It has recently been shown that the uterine cramps during menstruation can be as strong or at times even stronger than uterine contractions during labor! To think that women can carry on their daily business while enduring such intense monthly pain goes to prove what remarkable beings women really are.

Now that doctors and researchers have to admit that menstrual pain is real (they're getting around to discovering that about PMS, too), there is greater interest in learning how and why that pain is caused. Several theories are offered.

Dilation of the Cervix

One of the earliest theories as to the cause of menstrual distress is the dilation (opening) of the cervix. During menstruation the cervix must dilate to allow the menstrual flow to pass through. Since the cervix is highly sensitive, this stretching (similar to labor) causes pain. A blood clot passing through can cause excruciating pain.

It is thought that in some women the cervical opening is tight and must open that much more to allow the flow (or clots) to pass through. In some cases, the cervix may not dilate sufficiently at all, forcing some of the menstrual flow into the abdominal cavity, which could lead to endometriosis. (One symptom of endometriosis is marked abdominal pain several days before and/or during menstruation.) Therefore, a narrow cervix might very well explain why some women seem to experience much more pain than others.

A tight cervix may be due to anatomy or to a tense personality. (Endometriosis does occur more commonly in women who carry a good deal of anxiety or tension within them.)

To further support the cervical dilation theory, childbirth and having a D & C, both of which stretch the cervix, seem to alleviate menstrual cramping for many. However, some women with diagnosed narrow cervical canals do not experience severe menstrual pain and some women continue to have painful cramping even after giving birth.

Sensitivity to Progesterone

Another theory suggests that in some women the uterus is overly sensitive or even allergic to progesterone. The presence of progesterone in the second half of the cycle in some way activates the allergic reaction, resulting in painful cramping. In support of this theory is the common knowledge that when there is no ovulation, there is no corpus luteum, and therefore no progesterone is produced. Whether a cycle without ovulation results from oral contraceptives, certain hormone treatments, and/or other causes, there is usually little cramping. Some doctors feel that PMS is caused by a deficiency in progesterone, which may explain why some women who suffer from PMS do not report much menstrual pain.

To explain why childbirth often brings reduced spasmodic dysmenorrhea, it is postulated that during pregnancy, when high levels of progesterone are produced, the uterus becomes desensitized to it and therefore subsequent periods are not as painful.

Again, this theory does not account for women who have painful cramps after childbirth or while on the Pill. Nor does it explain why some women have both premenstrual and menstrual pain and discomfort. In addition, this theory does not answer why the cramps usually increase in intensity a few days before the period begins and peak the first day or so of menstruation—a time when progesterone levels are at their lowest. Sensitivity to progesterone, which results in uterine contractions, also contradicts the belief that progesterone acts as a relaxer, or an antispasmodic agent, on the uterus.

Prostaglandins

The most likely cause of menstrual pain may be prostaglandins, which are hormone-like substances that are found in nearly every cell of the human body. Some doctors suggest that prostaglandins are also responsible for many of the symptoms associated with PMS. So far, nine different groups of prostaglandins have been identified.

Prostaglandins work, in part, to cause contractions of the smooth, nonvoluntary muscles of the body, such as the blood vessels, the intestines, the heart, and the uterus. In medical use, prostaglandins are often injected to stimulate labor contractions and sometimes to induce abortion.

In recent years, it has been demonstrated that large amounts of prostaglandins are manufactured by the uterus just before and during the onset of menstruation. This could account for the cramping and body aches often felt premenstrually and during the first day or so of menstruation.

But why are prostaglandins produced by the uterus? In other words, why do we need this pain? Quite simply, the unused endometrial lining, or menstrual blood, must be shed each cycle so that a fresh lining can be created for the next egg. Prostaglandins produce the uterine contractions that are necessary to expel the unused uterine lining.

To further support the prostaglandin theory, recent studies have shown that women who experience intense menstrual pain have up to five times the amount of prostaglandins present in their menstrual flow as women who have only mild cramps. In addition, high levels of prostaglandins have been shown to cause nausea, irritability, water retention, and other PMS symptoms.

When an excess amount of prostaglandins is produced, the uterus contracts too much and too hard. The result is painful spasms and uterine cramps. Furthermore, the severely contracted uterine muscle compresses its own blood vessels and cuts off its blood supply, intensifying the pain.

Dr. Penny Wise Budoff, Clinical Associate Professor of Family Medicine at the State University of New York at Stony Brook, compares this situation to what happens when blood supply is cut off from the heart, or when the heart goes into spasms during a heart attack. We can all imagine how excruciating the pain (angina) must be. She further suggests that people might have a better understanding of menstrual pain if it were renamed "uterine angina."

Prostaglandins are also believed responsible for other symptoms associated with menstruation. Some of the prostaglandins produced by the uterus travel via the bloodstream and affect other nonvoluntary muscles. For example, the intestines are stimulated to contract quickly, causing diarrhea. In another example, blood vessels can suddenly constrict and then dilate, causing the sensation of dizziness and fainting. Furthermore, normal circulation may temporarily slow down, resulting in blood accumulation in the legs and feet, causing that heavy, sluggish feeling.

There has been substantial success in treating women with anti-prostaglandin agents. These medications have also been used with some degree of success in alleviating many PMS symptoms. This treatment and others will be explained later in this chapter.

Tipped Uterus

One popular theory can now be laid to rest. It was widely thought that a tipped uterus could cause severe menstrual pain. To correct this "condition," women were given exercises to do, devices were inserted into the vagina to force the uterus forward, even surgery was performed to reposition the uterus.

It is now known that at least 25 percent of women have a tipped uterus, and that there is no relationship between uterine position and menstrual pain.

Physical Disease and Disorder

Menstrual pain is occasionally caused by a physiological disease, disorder, or abnormality. (This is medically referred to as "secondary dysmenorrhea.") Endometriosis, fibroid tumors, polyps, pelvic inflammatory disease (PID), and other infections can often cause intense pain during menstruation, and in some instances before. Some PMS cases may actually be due to physiological disease.

Unfortunately, too many women wait too long before taking action when they have unusually severe menstrual pain. Often, the pain develops slowly, almost imperceptibly, over the months or years. Some women might also be exceptionally adept at coping with pain, and therefore their endurance develops along with the increasing cramps. Of course, other women may be frightened or embarrassed to see a doctor about a condition they believe will be considered imaginary or neurotic.

In truth, some gynecological disorders are difficult to diagnose. Therefore, if you see your doctor about severe cramping or PMS, a thorough physical examination should be performed. This might include a D & C and/or a laparoscopic examination (examining the pelvic cavity by means of a lighted viewing instrument).

If traditional treatments of spasmodic dysmenorrhea or premenstrual syndrome are not helping, insist on a thorough examination or find a doctor who will regard your pain more seriously.

The Shame of Menstruation

As we have seen, the menstrual cycle is healthy, natural, and normal. It is, in fact, a highly sophisticated means of ensuring the nurturance and support of a fertilized egg and thereby the reproduction of the human race.

Unfortunately, this normal biological event has been shrouded with myth, misinformation, and taboo. What is a natural process for the human female has been turned against her. Instead of viewing menstruation and premenstrual changes as part of the life-giving force, women see their menstrual flow as a source of shame.

Throughout the eons, in different cultures and times, it was believed that a menstruating woman could cause milk to spoil, wine to turn to vinegar, bees to die in their hives, cattle to miscarry, clocks to stop, natural disasters to occur. In various societies, she was excluded from social activities and was often forced into isolation during menstruation. Even today some myths persist—a woman must not swim or bathe during the menses, she shouldn't wash her hair, permanent waves will not "take," cakes will not bake properly, and fillings will fall out of teeth if put in during menstruation.

Religion, too, has played a powerful role in distorting a natural function, turning it into something that is thought of as evil, dirty, and harmful.

Hindu law forbids a woman to look at anybody, even her own children, "nor the light of the sun" during her menstrual period. Afterward she must bathe before she is fit to rejoin her family.

Some groups of people in India and other tribes around the world have banished menstruating women to specially built menstrual huts, where they may not speak to or look upon another person until their period is over.

Orthodox Judaism prescribes that after menstruation a woman must be cleansed in a ritual bath, called the "mikvah." Only after she is once again "clean" can she rejoin her husband in their marriage bed. Another Jewish custom, shared by several other cultures, is to slap the face of a daughter when she has her first period.

The Roman Catholic church also encourages abstinence during menstruation and generally reinforces the belief that "woman's pain" is punishment for Eve's involvement in the original sin.

In many Greek Orthodox communities, women are not allowed to partake of holy communion while menstruating.

The Bible contains a passage in the Old Testament that still holds the power to influence our thinking about menstruation.

> When a woman has her menstrual flow, she shall be in a state of impurity for seven days. Anyone who touches her shall be unclean until evening. Anything on which she lies or sits during her impurity shall be unclean. Anyone who touches her bed shall wash his garments, bathe in water, and be unclean until evening. Whoever touches any article of furni-

ture on which she is sitting, shall wash his garments, bathe in water, and be unclean until evening. But if she is on the bed or on the seat when he touches it, he shall be unclean until evening. If a man dares to be with her, he contracts her impurity and shall be unclean for seven days; every bed on which he then lies also becomes unclean.

—Leviticus 15:25-27

This overwhelming, prevailing negative attitude about menstruation is internalized by almost all women in our society. We see our bodies and their functions as shameful and disgusting. However liberated we may be, deep inside many women still feel unclean and impure when menstruating.

These feelings may or may not be conscious. As much as they might be suppressed or denied most of the month, an approaching period can cause those conflicted feelings to come closer to the surface. Some women are more sensitive to these cultural influences than others. And for various reasons, some women may not be able to overcome these inner conflicts as well as others.

The result may very well be the depression, hostility, and anxiety associated with premenstrual syndrome. Indeed, society's negative attitude is recognized by many psychiatrists and psychologists to be a contributing factor to the symptoms of PMS and the experience of pain during menstruation.

Menarche and Mothers

How your mother explained (or didn't explain) menstruation to you can influence your experience with premenstrual syndrome and pain during menstruation.

When a mother shares the information about menarche (the first menstrual period) with her young daughter in a way that creates self-respect and self-assurance in her developing female body, the benefits to that woman's life can be enormous. One of the most important gifts a mother can give her daughter is the love of being a woman and the joyous acceptance of her body. That profound and deeply laid foundation of self-acceptance can do a great deal of good in helping a woman cope with the physical aches and pain that normally accompany the menstrual cycle.

Sadly, too many women are left in ignorance, superstition, and negative feelings when it comes to menarche. Often, a girl will have her first period without even knowing what it is or that it is supposed to happen. And too many girls first learn about menstruation in terms of "the curse."

Lee M., 33, a newspaper editor, suffers from PMS and from menstrual cramps. She remembers vividly her first menstrual period.

> *I was eleven years old. Still in elementary school. One day I felt wet between my legs and discovered I was bleeding. I was horrified. If I had been bleeding from my arm or my chest, I would have told someone right away. But the blood was coming from "down there"—from my sexual parts. I was so ashamed. And terrified. There was so much blood and it didn't stop. I stuffed my panties with t-shirts and rags and then hid the bloodied clothes in the back of my closet. I didn't dare tell my mother. I was so certain I had done something wrong and was going to bleed to death as punishment. Finally, after three days, it stopped. I just hoped it wouldn't come back. Then my mother discovered the hidden clothes. She screamed at me and slapped me. She said that what I had was "the curse." Told me that now I could get into trouble with a man. I didn't understand what that meant or what the blood was or why it happened. All my mother said was that I shouldn't tell anybody about this and when it happened again, I should come to her and she would give me the right thing to use—sanitary napkins, as I learned later. The whole experience was filled with shame and mystery. I've never forgotten about it and I think about it every time my period is about to start.*

Susan H., 25, an executive assistant and a PMS sufferer, recounts how she learned about menstruation.

> *When I was about nine, I accidently went into the bathroom when my mother was changing a tampon. Of course, I didn't*

know what it was, but I saw the blood. My mother was very angry with me and said it was my fault, that I made her so tense she would bleed. Then she said the same thing was going to happen to me. Believe me, I was filled with dread for years, and when I was thirteen, it happened. Even though I had health classes that explained it all to me, I still connect my period with being bad.

Both Lee and Susan believe that their early negative experience with menstruation contributes to their emotional symptoms during their premenstrual days.

Indeed, many women are told about menstruation behind closed doors, in hushed voices, and are advised to keep this to themselves. This introduces the concept that menstruation is something that is not acceptable to other people, that it is not clean and not decent. It reinforces the belief that the functions of the female body are something to be ashamed of. This shame can continue, however subtly, throughout a lifetime.

No controlled study has been made to correlate the experience of menarche to PMS, but informal clinical observations by various doctors, psychologists, and counselors indicate that many women who are troubled with the more serious symptoms of PMS and have the most difficulty in coping with menstrual pain seem to be those women whose introduction to menstruation were confusing, disturbing, or frightening.

Menstruation and Self-Image

The menstrual cycle has enormous significance in a woman's life and in her perception of her self. The cyclical discomfort and pain that emanate from within the body hold significance beyond simple biology. The fact of the monthly menstrual flow, over which a woman has no conscious control takes on symbolic meaning.

Menstruation becomes a symbol for womanhood. Indeed, it serves to bring into the forefront of the mind that she is a woman.

Menstruation causes her to experience her womanliness very directly and in a deeply personal manner.

Man has nothing to compare with this experience. Perhaps in part this is why he is forever fighting to prove himself a man, prove his manhood, whereas a woman is secure in her knowledge of her womanhood. The changes that take place around the time of menstruation affirm her womanhood to the very depths of her being.

For this reason, women in general are far more aware of their bodies and the signals their bodies give them throughout the cycle and especially at PMS time. A woman can never quite forget or ignore her bodiliness in a way that a man often can.

Because of menstruation, women are also more conscious of their fertility and their inherent capacity for reproduction. We are more closely connected to the life-giving processes of pregnancy and birth. This profoundly affects our sexuality as well as self-perception.

To the woman who is content and happy in her body and accepting of her womanliness, the menstrual process, in spite of the physical pain, is a source of positive feelings in the pride of being a woman, of having a woman's body.

But for the woman who feels uncomfortable in her bodiliness, the coming event of menstrual flow will stir up emotions of frustration, powerlessness, and self-loathing. Many women who suffer from PMS report *hating* the feeling of being "out of control" of their bodies around the time of their periods. Some women feel betrayed by their bodies, which cause them so much pain and suffering. For them, menstruation and the premenstrual phase serve as a monthly symbol of the body, which is, on a very deep and profound level, found to be unacceptable.

This self-rejection is expressed by some women in premenstrual anxiety, moodiness, depression, and even thoughts of suicide. In other women, the time before the menses brings out feelings of hostility and rage. For still others, emotional problems can surface as a variety of physical symptoms. This is the darker, hidden side of PMS, one that some people would prefer to overlook in their search for a quick medical cure.

How a woman adjusts to and accepts the fact of menstruation and all that it encompasses plays an extremely important role in self-image, and therefore in the way she perceives the bodily changes that accompany the menstrual cycle, especially those just prior to menstruation.

Menstruation and the Mind

Most PMS and menstrual problems are interwoven with a woman's psyche and her emotions. Actually, this can be said about every physical problem. It is well known that a physical problem can lead to an emotional one just as an emotional one can cause a physical one. Every physical problem carries a strong psychological component for all people.

There is a growing number of members of the medical community who feel that almost all physical conditions, from the common cold to cancer, are closely connected to the mind.

Some might disagree with the breadth of the statement, but it may well contain a large grain of truth. In many cases, there are factors in a person's personality that find release in a weaker part of that person's body. For example, an emotional problem can surface as a stomach ulcer in one person, migraine headaches in another, heart disease in a third, and menstrual problems in still another. Often, the physical problem occurs indirectly as a result of behavior or life style, which are, of course, also linked to an individual's psyche.

Does this mean that PMS and menstrual pain are psychosomatic after all? Unfortunately, the answer is not black and white as some people might like to have it. The complex interrelationship between PMS and personality will be explored more fully in Chapter 6.

Men and Menstruation

Women are most directly affected by the menstrual cycle as well as the psychological and sociological factors that often go hand in hand with this biological event. But men, too, are affected by menstruation. The knowledge that women menstruate becomes a part their lives and influences their personality and behavior, especially in relationships with women.

We discussed how early experiences with menstruation can affect a woman. The same could be said for a man. If he was told about menstruation in a loving manner by his parents, in such a way that he understood the physical process and his own special role in reproduction (that is, the life force), chances are he will regard women with respect and caring.

Unfortunately, most boys learn about menstruation in the same haphazard way as do most girls. Often boys learn about the menstrual cycle through dirty jokes or misinformation passed on by other boys. Or a boy might discover it accidentally through his mother or an older sister. The sight of menstrual blood, or hearing about women "bleeding down there," can fill a young boy with horror, fear, or revulsion. This can carry through his lifetime and profoundly influence his perceptions of and relationships with women.

Many men are deeply uncomfortable with the fact of menstruation. This probably stems from early associations with blood, injury, sickness, and death.

A few socio-anthropologists believe that in ancient civilizations women were worshipped for their ability to bleed without bodily harm and for the miraculous power to give birth. But since the forces behind these biological events were not understood, they instilled fear. If a woman could create life she might also have the power to destroy. And so to control those powers and those who possessed them, menstruating women were ostracized from normal participation in society.

Some psychoanalytic theories hold that the fear of menstruation is rooted in the "castration complex." In simple terms, a man sees (or knows of) blood flowing from a woman's sexual organs. He cannot imagine this happening to him unless some injury (or castration) were to occur to his genitals. Psychoanalytically speaking, he fails to regard women as complete human beings, but sees them rather as castrated men. His ego therefore builds a defense mechanism against the horror that he might be castrated and die.

He may reason (consciously or unconsciously) that women have been punished for being bad or evil and were castrated.

Hence, the fear of castration is projected onto the woman and menstruation becomes a taboo. In part, this explains the many myths and practices associated with menstruation. By controlling the menstruating woman (by isolating her in a menstrual hut or by keeping her out of the work force), men attempt to control their own fear of castration, blood, and death.

In very practical terms, men and women rarely discuss menstruation. In fact, most men are woefully unaware of why it happens, what is taking place inside a woman's body, and how the monthly cycle affects them.

Couples sometime begin this discussion when it comes to deciding on sexual activity during menstruation. A few studies have shown that over half of men and women abstain from sex for the several days around the menses. One study indicated that men are almost twice as likely to object to sex during menstruation as are women.

Of course, there are several factors to consider. A heavy flow may discourage some couples. Quite a few women report little sexual desire on those days when they are in most pain.

When both partners are in agreement, there is little conflict, but when one partner wants sexual intercourse and the other does not, serious problems in the relationship can develop, especially when there are other underlying factors.

Some couples overcome the simpler mechanical problems of sex during menstruation by the woman's using a diaphragm or a menstrual cup, which catches the flow and keeps it from the vagina during intercourse. Other couples try alternative means of sexual play to achieve orgasm.

Many times, a woman desires sex during menstruation because she feels greater arousal at that time. Sometimes, though, a woman needs the reassurance that she is still desirable and acceptable even though she is menstruating.

In general, a man can help his partner by giving her extra affection and showing that he continues to cherish her during her premenstrual phase and during menstruation.

Ronnie J., 29, a screenwriter, tells how her husband helped.

> *I've always had very bad feelings about myself as a woman. I guess I was one who thought getting your period was something awful. But my husband has such a healthy attitude about it. When he wants to make love and I'm too ashamed because of the blood, he tells me, "I want you to know that I love you when you are having your period and when you're not. I love you because you are a woman and I love every part of your womanhood." I'm smiling just remembering this because after four years of marriage, I'm beginning to love my womanhood, too.*

Twelve Ways to Treat Menstrual Pain

There are many methods of treating menstrual pain. Some of them are age-old, others are just discovered and can be obtained by prescription through your doctor.

Unfortunately, there is still no way to banish menstrual cramps totally and forever, but there are several remedies that can at least lessen the pain and make for a more comfortable period. Many of these methods can also reduce PMS discomfort.

Not all of the following may work for you, but a few might. In most cases, you can try combining the methods—or you may come up with your own individual formula for alleviating menstrual pain.

1. One of the oldest and most popular methods is *heat* applied to the lower abdomen. A hot-water bottle or a heating pad is often used for this purpose. Some women find placing the hot-water bottle or heating pad on their lower back is effective. Try moving the heat source to find the place most comfortable for you. One woman said she used two heating pads, one for her abdomen and one for her lower back. "That way, I get twice the relief!"

Some women might feel guilty about crawling into bed with a heating pad. But this is not just pampering yourself. There is a medical reason why heat works. It is known that muscles in spasm (the uterus is a muscle and spasms are felt as cramps) respond to heat by relaxing. Therefore, the cramps become less severe. This method is perfectly safe and relatively inexpensive. Beware of burns, however. Never place an uncovered heating pad on bare skin.

2. Another technique is to rub the abdomen with *deep-heating oils and creams.* There are many such products available at any drugstore. Many deep-heating salves are marketed as products to relieve arthritis or muscular aches, but for some women they also provide relief from menstrual cramps. No prescription is needed, but follow the manufacturer's instructions.

3. Sometimes, simply *massaging* the affected area can prove helpful. Massaging creates heat and also promotes blood circulation. You can massage your own abdomen or have someone else give you a massage. (Be sure to have him or her begin gently. Work together to find the best movements and pressure for you.) Another successful technique is to massage the lower back with the fingertips. This seems to create a slight numbing sensation and can provide considerable relief while the massaging takes place.

4. Other women find that taking a *hot bath* can ease menstrual cramps. Contrary to popular belief, there is no danger in bathing during menstruation. The heat relaxes the muscles and may serve to help open the cervix, thereby relieving cramps. (Do not wear a tampon while bathing. In fact, some gynecologists recommend using sanitary napkins instead of tampons during the hours or days when the spasms are most severe.) Avoid sitting in excessively hot water, which may cause nausea, a feeling of weakness, or fainting spells.

5. Some women find that *drinking hot liquids* produces a soothing effect. Taking heat into the body works in much the same way as heat applied to the body. Clear broths, light soups, coffee, tea, hot chocolate, and herbal teas are often used for this purpose.

A word about herbal teas: Herbal or "natural" remedies are very popular today. Although there is no scientific proof of their effectiveness, some women swear by various herbs, including chamomile, dandelion, elder bark, ginseng, raspberry, and valerian. Most of these work as mild diuretics and probably are psychologically calming and relaxing. However, just because herbs are natural, many of them do have powerful pharmacological properties when taken in large quantities or when mixed with other substances. They can cause nausea, illness, and even death. As with anything, use herbal teas in moderation.

6. Yet another common home remedy for menstrual cramps is drinking *alcoholic beverages.* In fact, many of the elixirs used in the past to treat menstrual distress contained liberal quantities of alcohol. Today, some women find that a glass of wine, sherry, or brandy, hot tea with whiskey or rum, or even a stiff shot of liquor can ease their menstrual cramps. It is known that alcohol works to relax uterine cramping. Alcohol also has a sedative effect. For this reason, it is indeed a "home" remedy—to be used at home when you have the opportunity to relax. Do not attempt to drive, tend to small children, or go to work while using alcohol. Also, be aware of your own tolerance level, which might be reduced during the days around the menses. Too much alcohol can cause nausea and dizziness. This method is obviously not appropriate for young teenagers and for those who have problems with substance abuse. In addition, alcohol should not be mixed with various drugs or medications. Alcohol cannot be considered a medically approved treatment for menstrual pain.

7. Another effective method to reduce menstrual pain is *sleep.* Many women report that after taking a nap they feel much better, their cramps are less severe, and they have more energy. Rest is, of course, one of the best ways for relaxing the mind and the body's muscles. After a good night's sleep, most women awaken to find their cramps are considerably reduced or have vanished altogether.

8. An enjoyable method of reducing cramping is through *orgasm.* There is a medical reason for this—orgasm relaxes the uterus and promotes the blood flow in that area. If you feel uncomfortable about having sex with your partner at this time, you might try masturbation. If you need to, simply tell your partner or your family that you'll be taking a nap. This will afford you the privacy you need. In fact, here is an excellent opportunity to combine two methods, having an orgasm and following it with a relaxing nap.

9. *Exercise* can also reduce menstrual cramping. There are several exercises that strengthen the abdominal muscles and promote circulation. Yoga can also provide some relief during menstrual

cramping. You can learn more about these exercises through books or classes. In general, it seems to pay to be physically in shape. Although there may be no medical correlation between menstrual relief and exercise, it is commonly recognized that dancers and athletes rarely have painful dysmenorrhea and usually do not suffer from PMS.

10. There are a number of *over-the-counter drugs* that work especially well for menstrual pain. Some of the most popular are Femcaps, Midol, Pamprin, and Trandar. These and other such products usually contain a compound of aspirin or acetaminophen, caffeine, or another mild diuretic, and one or two other ingredients that act as antispasmodics.

In addition, there are other nonprescription products that many women swear by. They include Humphreys No. 11 tablets and Lydia Pinkham's tonics or tablets. Both contain extracts of various herbs and plants, such as cimicifuga, dogwood, and licorice. Although their value has not been proven and their effectiveness has been questioned, countless women have used these products and have gained relief from monthly pain.

Surprisingly enough, probably the best nonprescription medication to use for relief of menstrual cramps is simple aspirin. Although it has been around since 1915, scientists are only now beginning to understand how aspirin works. Actually, it is quite a powerful drug. If it were introduced today the Federal Food and Drug Administration would undoubtedly classify it as a prescription medicine!

Aspirin can reduce fever, pain, and inflammation. Aspirin also works as an anticoagulant and prevents the formation of clots. Blood clots formed in the uterus can be painful when passing through the cervical opening. Just recently, it was discovered that aspirin inhibits the production of prostaglandins, the major cause of menstrual related pain and the possible cause of some premenstrual discomfort. Many women do find their cramps are more tolerable after they take aspirin, but sometimes aspirin just doesn't seem to be enough. However effective aspirin is, it cannot totally halt all prostaglandin production. Stronger anti-prostaglandin medications may be needed. Such drugs are now available by prescription and will be described shortly.

To prevent the buildup of prostaglandins, some doctors recommend taking aspirin several days before the onset of menstruation. Taken during the premenstrual period, aspirin can also help alleviate some PMS symptoms.

Excessive use of aspirin can lead to indigestion, heartburn, and stomach ulceration or bleeding. Some people cannot use aspirin—for example, those suffering from ulcers or other gastric disorders, and those who are allergic to it. If aspirin does not agree with you, there are several aspirin-like products available. Their generic name is acetaminophen. One brand name is Tylenol.

11. When self-help and over-the-counter treatments fail to reduce menstrual pain, many women turn to their physicians for help through *prescription drugs*. There are many available and some of them are very potent in eliminating cramps.

But let's begin by looking at several common prescriptive medicines that are controversial in the treatment of menstrual cramps. Many doctors prescribe tranquilizers and sedatives for women. Although these drugs may relieve anxiety, they do not treat menstrual cramps. An increasing number of gynecologists state that such drugs as Valium and Librium are not effective in reducing uterine spasms.

Other popularly prescribed pain medications are codeine, Darvon, and Percodan. However, doctors who have conducted studies as to their effectiveness have found that aspirin is superior on almost all counts. Aspirin is also far less costly and carries fewer side effects.

Birth-control pills are probably the most effective prescribed treatment for spasmodic dysmenorrhea. Oral contraceptives may be even more effective than the new anti-prostaglandin drugs; however, the Pill does alter natural hormonal production and may not be acceptable to some patients for various reasons.

Oral contraceptives prevent ovulation and hence the production of progesterone. This results in menstrual periods that are not painful. Furthermore, since there is less buildup of the uterine lining, the menstrual flow is reduced, which may account for less painful cramping. It is also thought that reduced hormone production may prevent prostaglandin production.

There are well-publicized side effects associated with the Pill, even though it is considered safe for the majority of women, especially those under 35 who do not smoke. Although some women find relief from PMS symptoms when on the Pill, it can worsen the symptoms in other women. Therefore, the possible risks of this treatment must be weighed against the possible benefits. Your doctor will need a careful description of your symptoms before he or she can accurately prescribe this method. Be sure to ask about the numerous possible side effects, both physical and emotional. Contact your doctor immediately if you feel you are incurring any of them.

Other hormonal treatments have included synthetic progesterone and male hormones, called androgens. These have been used with various degrees of success, but because of numerous side effects, they are not generally recommended for spasmodic dysmenorrhea.

Antispasmodic drugs such as Librax and Inderal, have been used to treat menstrual cramps, but they have not been studied for their effectiveness in specifically relieving spasmodic dysmenorrhea.

Recently, several anti-prostaglandins drugs have been shown to be very effective in treating menstrual pain. When they were first approved for use, they were heralded as a godsend for women with intense menstrual pain. Indeed, studies have shown that up to 80 or 90 percent of women using these medications report remarkable relief.

Prostaglandin-inhibiting drugs work by blocking the production of prostaglandins. They are more effective than aspirin in doing so. Currently, there are several such drugs available by prescription. In many ways they are safer than the Pill in that they do not disturb normal hormonal fluctuations and are only taken one to three days a month, so the chance for long-term side effects is reduced. However, short-term side effects are common and may affect up to 60 percent of those taking these drugs. Therefore, they are usually not recommended unless the pain is severe and is not alleviated by more traditional methods.

Because this medication is receiving such wide attention and has been used for treating both premenstrual and menstrual pain, the pros and cons of the new anti-prostaglandin drugs will be explored in the following section.

12. Finally, a few women who can find no relief from any other treatment turn to *surgery* to relieve extreme menstrual pain.

Often, a physical abnormality or disorder can be corrected by surgery, thereby eliminating the cause of the pain for that individual woman.

One common operation is the D & C (dilation and curettage), in which the cervix is widened (dilated) and gently scraped with a special instrument (a curette). The scraped tissue is removed from the uterus and then sent to a laboratory for examination. In this way, a physician can diagnose certain physical causes for the painful symptoms.

As already mentioned, the D & C in itself often alleviates the pain for many women.

Anesthesia is used in this procedure and therefore it carries some risk. In addition, there is always the chance of complication, as in any surgical procedure. In itself, a D & C cannot be considered a permanent cure since cramps usually return after a period of time.

A very effective surgical technique consists of severing nerve passageways that carry pain sensations from the uterus. This procedure is called presacral neurectomy. Afterward, pain is no longer felt as a result of uterine cramping. Again, general anesthesia must be used and therefore the procedure carries some risk in addition to the chance of complications. Occasionally there is damage to the sensory fibers of the bladder, leading to a loss of control of the bladder. For these reasons, this operation should be performed only in the most extreme cases.

The New Prostaglandin-Inhibiting Drugs

If you are one of the several million women who are totally incapacitated by menstrual pain or if your cramps are so overwhelming that they greatly interfere with your work, there is now a way that may end your suffering. The new prostaglandin-inhibiting drugs are extremely effective in most women who cannot find success in other methods of treating menstrual pain. If you suffer primarily from premenstrual pain, these drugs may also prove effective in relieving some of your physical symptoms.

In order to obtain these drugs, you must see your doctor and get a prescription. Most gynecologists are aware of them and may recommend this treatment for you.

There are five anti-prostaglandin drugs currently being used to treat painful spasmodic dysmenorrhea. They are Anaprox, Motrin, Nalfon 200, Naprosyn, and Ponstel.

One drug may work better for you than another. Therefore, if the one your doctor prescribes does not seem effective or causes unpleasant side effects, you may be given a different type. In some cases it may take two or three cycles before the drug works with greatest effectiveness.

As with any prescriptive drug, use it only as directed by your physician and notify him or her immediately if you suffer any side effects, especially headaches, difficulty in breathing, itching, or skin rash.

Some people may not be able to use the prostaglandin-inhibiting drugs. The contraindications include aspirin allergy, diabetes, kidney disease, asthma, ulcers, heart disease, hypertension, gastrointestinal inflammation, liver disease, and bleeding disorders. Be sure to tell your physician of any medications—whether prescription or over-the-counter—that you are taking.

A few words of caution: the drugs may cause drowsiness in some people and therefore driving and working with dangerous machinery should be avoided. In addition, never take aspirin while using these drugs.

In general, the major side effects include an upset stomach, heartburn, nausea, constipation, vomiting, diarrhea, headache, dizziness, irritability, depression, drowsiness, sleeplessness, and the inability to think clearly. In addition, there is not enough evidence yet to determine how these drugs affect a developing fetus, therefore they should not be used if there is the possibility of pregnancy. A more complete listing of anti-prostaglandin medicines and their particular side effects can be found in Chapter 9.

Since the drugs are usually taken only for a short period of time, the several days around the menses, serious side effects are less likely to be experienced.

The menstrual cycle has many physical and psychological overtones. Menstruation is more than just a biological event. It is an important part of being a woman. How a woman views herself as a biological female does affect the way she perceives the changes that occur in her body and her emotions throughout the menstrual cycle.

The important thing to remember is that changes *do* take place—and they affect our bodies and our emotions. As women, we need to give ourselves more credit for the way we handle these changes. It is doubtful whether the average man could cope nearly as well.

Although most women go through painful days during their premenstrual and menstrual periods, we usually have only ourselves to count on for support during this time. And this can be a lonely time, a time when we don't dare talk about our pain, for fear that it will be dismissed as "women's complaints," or that we will be thought of as somehow inferior.

Yet we go to work, take care of children, cook meals, tend to husband/boyfriend, carry on chores, do the best possible to provide the love and support needed—all the while enduring pain that may be as severe as labor contractions or coronary angina. And often, no one even knows.

5

YOUR BODY AND BIOLOGY

The Physiology of PMS

I don't suffer from depression or mood swings the way some women do. My symptoms seem to be more physical —bloating, painful breasts, cramping, exhaustion. But I have to admit, when I get this way, I tend to feel far more irritable. I just feel out of sorts with myself.

Elena P., 42
Real estate agent

The Physical Symptoms of PMS

Of the women who experience PMS effects, most have at least some physical symptoms. As we mentioned earlier, physical problems can make you feel edgy and upset. Countless people have probably shared the thought, "If only I felt better physically, I know my mood would improve, too." This chapter will identify the major physical symptoms of PMS, explain their origins, and provide ways to overcome premenstrual discomfort.

In general, it can be said that the way you experience the physical symptoms of PMS largely depends on your individual body chemistry. No two people are exactly alike—the hormonal fluctuations that are part of the menstrual cycle are highly individualistic. And a particular woman's psyche can influence her experience and perception of PMS, as well. This accounts for the wide variety of physical symptoms associated with PMS. The way PMS affects you might be very different from its effect on another woman.

The only factor held in common is that the physical symptoms begin sometime after ovulation and end around the onset of menstruation.

This is an important point to reiterate. In diagnosing PMS, you must be careful to keep a chart (see chapter 2) of your symptoms and know that they appear only premenstrually. If your symptoms occur at other times in the month, they may indicate a physiological disease or disorder that should be brought to your doctor's attention.

If a particular PMS symptom, whether it be bloating or hives, is worrying you or causing undue pain and discomfort, you should consult your physician. He or she may be able to give you reassurance that nothing serious is wrong and/or provide you with appropriate treatment.

The most common of the physical premenstrual symptoms happen to millions of menstruating women. But there is no reason why they should stop you from enjoying your life and doing what you want to do. Whatever your symptoms might be, you are not alone, you are not imagining them, and most likely your symptoms are normal and can be treated.

Fluid Retention

Among the most common symptoms of PMS is fluid/salt retention. In fact, some doctors believe this to be the underlying cause of premenstrual syndrome.

Why water and salt are retained premenstrually is not yet fully understood. It is thought that progesterone promotes fluid retention. Progesterone is present only during the second half, or luteal phase, of the menstrual cycle. Some believe that estrogen also promotes water retention.

It is known that excessive fluid retention during the premenstrual period (also called cyclical edema) can cause swelling in the abdomen, breasts, genitals, ankles, feet, hands, and even the brain. This is a possible reason for the headaches and migraines suffered by many women with PMS. Abdominal swelling is usually the result of water being retained in the bowel wall, which can cause diarrhea or constipation, two of the more unpleasant PMS symptoms.

Some women notice a restlessness or an inability to stay still in one position for long. During the premenstrual time, fluid (including blood) tends to accumulate in the legs and feet, accounting for that heavy feeling. At the same time, blood is drained from the upper body and brain, which may result in a general feeling of weakness, numbness, light-headedness, giddiness, dizziness, and fainting.

During PMS time, some women feel unusually thirsty or have a craving for salty foods. You may have noticed a decrease in urinary output during premenstrual days—then a sudden increase the day before or the day of your menstrual period. Marnie L., 38, a secretary, swears she can predict the day her period will begin because "exactly one day before, I'm constantly running to the bathroom."

Some of the other physical symptoms associated with fluid retention include uncomfortable feelings of general fatigue, dullness, and bloatedness.

Fluid retention may be responsible for emotional changes as well, such as tension, mood swings, depression, lethargy, fatigue, anger, and anxiety.

To some degree, all women tend to retain fluid and salt premenstrually. One survey shows about 30 percent of women experience weight gain of one to three pounds. Rarely do women gain more than five pounds, but cases have been recorded of women who have gained ten, fifteen, and even twenty pounds in the two weeks prior to menstruation. Some women have a second set of clothes to wear during PMS week.

Why some women retain more fluid than others is in part explained by individual differences in physical and chemical make-up. Premenstrual fluid retention has been studied by a number of researchers, but without consistent results. Some studies find no weight gain at all in women during the premenstrual period. Other studies show just the opposite. To account for the feeling of bloatedness and related symptoms when there is little or no actual weight gain, some researchers hypothesize that bodily fluids *shift* to the abdomen and other affected sites.

The dietary habits of women with PMS have also been studied, particularly by Drs. G. S. Goei and G. E. Abraham along with scientist J. L. Ralston in California. They found that women with premenstrual syndrome consumed twice as much table salt (sodium) as did women without PMS. The high amount of salt used by these PMS patients might explain their problems associated with periodic water retention.

Diuretics are sometimes taken by women for relief of premenstrual bloating. Dr. Jerome Hoffman, who conducted a study in Florida that demonstrated a definite weight gain in women suffering from PMS, found that the use of diuretics not only decreased the amount of weight gain but also relieved many other PMS symptoms.

The use of diet and/or diuretics to treat PMS is controversial, primarily because there is still so much disagreement about the actual causes of the condition. However, many doctors recommend that women begin a simple and safe treatment by reducing their fluid and salt intake starting around the time of ovulation, or between 10 and 14 days before the expected onset of the next period. Many women notice marked improvement after following this change in dietary habits.

Sometimes a mild diuretic (water pills) may help alleviate water retention during the premenstrual days. In more severe cases of PMS, a mild tranquilizer may be prescribed along with a diuretic to be taken for about a week before menstruation.

Like any medication, diuretics have side effects. The most common can cause a depletion of potassium, which can lead to weakness, muscle aches, cramps, spasms, and, in extreme cases, death. To prevent this, doctors recommend eating potassium-rich foods, especially bananas, dried or fresh apricots, orange juice, and tomatoes. Your doctor may also recommend a supplement of potassium tablets.

In treating PMS, diuretics should never be used every day of the cycle. Overuse or long-term use of these drugs can lead to a physiological alteration in the way the body naturally flushes out water. Never exceed dosages prescribed by your physician. Check with your doctor right away if you notice any side effects.

Over-the-counter and prescriptive diuretics will be described more fully in chapters 8 and 9.

A related theory as to the cause of PMS is the lack of potassium, often noted in women during the premenstrual days. Some doctors feel that too much fluid in relation to potassium levels may lead to premenstrual syndrome symptoms. In general, eating potassium-rich foods seems to dispel weakness, lethargy, and irritability.

If you feel you suffer from fluid retention, keep a daily chart of your weight. You might want to add this information to your premenstrual chart in chapter 2. This might prove valuable should you decide to make an appointment with your doctor for a prescriptive diuretic.

Although a change of diet and the use of diuretics help many women, in others only some of the symptoms disappear. For a few women, diet and diuretics provide no relief. Since PMS might be caused by any number of factors, fluid retention may not be the answer for everyone.

If you suffer from PMS, a reduced salt diet, possibly combined with a diuretic, may mark the beginning of controlling your premenstrual symptoms. It did for Tracy C., 44, a stockbroker.

> *I had all the symptoms of premenstrual fluid retention —swollen abdomen, painful breasts, feeling sluggish, bloated, headaches, tension, and tiredness. Really, I was a wreck for about a week before my period started! It seemed to me that it was getting worse over the years, so I finally went to my general practitioner. I was lucky. He recognized PMS right away and suggested I cut out salt two weeks before menstruation. He also gave me a diuretic to use on the really bad days. Ever since then, PMS time has been much easier. I feel alive and active all month long.*

Low Blood Sugar

One of the most common symptoms of PMS is the craving for sweet and/or starchy foods. During the premenstrual week, many women feel an intense desire for candies, chocolates, cakes, cookies, pastries, or anything that is sweet and sticky. Other women report an increased appetite for pasta, breads, potato chips, and other high carbohydrate foods. Sometimes there is a craving for both sweet and salty foods.

Mary-Lynn K., 30, a marketing manager for a cosmetics firm, says she knows when it's PMS time when she catches herself "sitting in front of the television set with a box of M&M's in one hand and a bag of potato chips in the other."

These cravings are often caused by low blood sugar, or hypoglycemia. Hypoglycemia occurs when sugar is metabolized too quickly, usually as the result of an imbalance of the ratio of insulin to blood sugar.

Although some individuals suffer from chronic, or continuous, low blood sugar, many women with PMS experience this condition only during the premenstrual days. In this case, it is called periodic hypoglycemia. Following the start of menstruation, blood-sugar metabolism returns to normal and the cravings for sweets and starches cease.

No one knows for certain why the premenstrual phase brings on bouts of low blood sugar, but most doctors feel it is related to hormonal fluctuations. Progesterone seems to lower blood-sugar levels. One study showed a marked increase in the number of insulin receptors during the second half of the menstrual cycle. Too much insulin can cause lowered levels of blood sugar.

Many of the symptoms associated with hypoglycemia are also associated with premenstrual syndrome. Some doctors believe PMS can be directly attributed to low blood sugar.

The physical symptoms include fatigue, fainting, dizziness, weakness, sweating, headaches, migraines, exhaustion, nausea, gastrointestinal complaints, and the familiar craving for sweets.

Several emotional reactions associated with hypoglycemia are also linked with PMS. They are nervousness, anxiety, depression, impulsiveness, irritability, aggressiveness, and even antisocial behavior. Some doctors believe that low blood sugar can trigger criminal behavior.

How aggressiveness, hostility, and violent behavior are related to hypoglycemia (and PMS) is still unclear. One theory holds that low blood sugar affects the brain in such a way as to lower inhibitions.

That some women experience only mild symptoms of periodic hypoglycemia and others suffer from its more severe manifestations is attributed to individual differences in body chemistry along with individual personality factors.

In general though, it seems that women who suffer from PMS tend to have poorer eating and nutritional habits. The research team of Dr. Goei, Mr. Ralston, and Dr. Abraham has found that women who suffer from PMS eat three times the amount of sugar and twice the amount of carbohydrates as other women. Furthermore, they observed that women with severe PMS symptoms take in more calories per day than women with few PMS symptoms.

The premenstrual days are a time when women need especially good nutrition. Unfortunately, many women care for themselves very poorly during the premenstrual period.

Some women who experience bloating may panic at their weight gain and go on a severe diet. Conversely, other women may feel so low in energy and emotional reserves that they binge on cookies, cakes, chocolates, etc. Worse yet, some women binge one day and feel so regretful that they go on a total fast the next day, only to be overwhelmed with exhaustion and craving so they overeat again the following day. Such practices can seriously disrupt normal metabolism and can worsen the symptoms of PMS.

To combat low blood sugar and the symptoms associated with it and PMS, many doctors and nutritionists recommend eating "little and often." This means having small meals five or six times a day rather than two or three hearty ones. A nutritious breakfast is a must. At midmorning, have a snack such as fresh fruit. Eat a small, light lunch and follow with a second snack midafternoon. Eat a sensible dinner and have another snack an hour or so before going to bed. This method of eating will help keep your blood sugar at a steady level throughout the day. Try to eat foods that are high in protein and low in carbohydrates and fats. Lean meats, fish, milk, eggs, cheese, yogurt, and unsalted nuts are especially recommended. In addition, fresh fruits and fresh vegetables should round out your nutritional needs.

Avoid empty calories, such as potato chips, soda pop, presweetened and artifically sweetened foods. Cigarettes and alcohol can also affect blood-sugar levels; therefore, use these substances with moderation if at all. In any case, fasting should not be done during the premenstrual phase if you suffer from PMS.

If you are on a diet to lose weight and you have PMS, you should probably not attempt to shed pounds during the premenstrual days. If you do put on a few pounds premenstrually, try not to be too hard on yourself. The weight gain is probably due to water retention and will most likely disappear after your period starts. Think of the premenstrual days as marking time until you can safely begin to lose weight again.

What about those times when you have an overwhelming desire for chocolate brownies or mounds of spaghetti? Some doctors would say such foods should be strictly avoided, but realistically, some starches and sweets may help pick up your energy and your spirits while fulfilling the craving. Most women with PMS can safely allow themselves a little indulgence, especially when their nutritional needs are well met by a high protein diet. But the key word is *little*—enjoy such treats in moderation.

Maybe, instead of the usual diets that never work, what we really need is "The PMS Diet"—a diet that takes into account the physical and emotional needs of women during the premenstrual time. A suggested start for this special diet can be found in Chapter 8.

Of course, nutrition is not a cure-all for any condition, but low blood sugar may trigger PMS symptoms and may be the underlying cause of the symptoms for many women.

The symptoms of PMS may be a signal that the body needs extra care and nutrition at this time. All women would do well to pay attention to their physical needs, and to provide themselves with good nutrition and sound eating habits in order to promote better health and a feeling of well-being during the premenstrual days.

Painful Breasts

Many women with premenstrual syndrome find that their worst physical symptom is breast pain. This pain can range from slight tenderness to moderate discomfort to extreme pain. Some women an barely wear clothing around their breasts. The affectionate hugs from children are excruciating. Love-making becomes almost impossible. For a few women, the pain radiates out to the entire chest area, armpits, and upper arms.

This is one symptom that brings many women to their gynecologist's office. If you have ever felt a painful lump or thickening in one of your breasts, your first thought may have been "Cancer..."

You're not alone. Many women who examine their breasts in the week or so before menstruation discover lumps, nodules, or cysts. Often the breasts feel granular or fibrous. Most of the swelling and pain occur around the upper portion of the breast, where most glandular tissue is located, and around the nipple. One breast may be more painful than the other. Furthermore, the lumps, their position, the breasts' texture, and the degree of discomfort can vary from month to month. In most cases, the symptoms disappear with the onset of menstruation.

What is going on here? What are those lumps?

This condition is called fibrocystic breast disease (FBD). Although it carries an ominous sounding name, FBD is usually benign and does not indicate a serious abnormality.

In fact, FBD is extremely common. At least 25 percent of menstruating women have it and some physicians would say that virtually all women over 35 experience it to some degree. The condition disappears completely after menopause.

Actually, fibrocystic breast disease is a result of normal monthly hormonal changes. Just as the lining of the uterus responds to the presence of progesterone, the breasts also respond by beginning to prepare for milk production. Progesterone triggers the growth of glandular, duct, and fibrous tissue in the breasts. If no pregnancy occurs, these newly grown glands and tissues break down and are reabsorbed into the body.

The discomfort and pain occur when the breakdown and/or the reabsorption processes are not working properly. Sometimes there is excessive growth of tissue that cannot all be reabsorbed. In any case, small pockets of the no longer needed cells and secretions manifest themselves as lumps or cysts.

Even with this knowledge, a woman finding any kind of lump

might think, "This is it. I have breast cancer." If you check your breasts regularly, there are a few ways you can tell the difference between normal breast changes and a more serious breast disease.

First, most lumps, nodules, or cysts that are cyclical—that is, they come and go according to the menstrual cycle—are *not* cancerous. Cancerous tumors rarely fluctuate in size and do not move around to different locations from month to month.

Second, although premenstrual cysts can be firm or hard, they are usually soft and are usually movable within the breast tissue. Cancerous tumors tend to be hard and cannot be separated or moved from the surrounding breast tissue.

Third, cysts usually hurt, breast cancer tumors usually do not.

To avoid the natural confusion—and fear—that often results from a breast self-examination, check your breasts once per cycle, *about seven days after the start of your menstrual period*. This is a time when swelling has lessened and hormone levels are still low.

Breast cancer has several symptoms of which you should be aware. Contact your doctor immediately if you notice any of the following:

- An area of the breast that is depressed or bulging.
- A part of the breast that feels warm or hot to the touch, especially if accompanied by thickening.
- The appearance of dilated veins on the breasts.
- The appearance of areas on the breasts that have the texture of an orange peel; or any change of texture, shape, or color of the breasts.
- Changes in the shape, size, texture, or direction of the nipple.
- Discharge from the nipple, cracks in the nipple, scaling of the skin around the nipple.
- A lump in the armpit.
- A sore on the breast or nipple that does not heal.
- Any unusual ache or pain that persists and is not related to the menstrual cycle.

There has been some dispute over the link between fibrocystic breast disease (FBD) and cancer. Some doctors believe there is no correlation between the two while others hold that a woman with FBD is up to four times as likely to develop breast cancer. One of the contributing reasons may be the possibility of cancer developing amidst the other cysts and nodules—a cancerous tumor that might be missed by the average women.

To be on the safe side, a woman with breast cysts should see her gynecologist for a breast examination twice a year, especially if she is over 35. A physician can usually distinguish the difference between benign cysts and possible malignant growths.

Although many women continue to suffer from monthly breast pain, there are measures you can take to alleviate this PMS symptom effectively.

Most gynecologists recommend as a first step to eliminate from your diet all foods that contain the chemical methylxanthine (or xanthine). It is thought that methylxanthines stimulate breast cells to overproduce tissue and fluids, which may aggravate FBD symptoms.

The best-known and most often consumed methylxanthine is caffeine. Caffeine is found in coffee, tea, cola drinks, some other soft drinks, chocolate, and several over-the-counter medications.

Many studies and clinical observations have confirmed that eliminating caffeine from the diet works to alleviate FBD. The relief lasts as long as caffeine is avoided. The painful cysts return when caffeine consumption is resumed.

Cathy E., 39, an art instructor, relates her experience:

I had noticed a lump and a fibrous feeling in my right breast that kept coming back. After several months, I decided I had better call my doctor. Trembling, I telephoned her, expecting her to say that I must come in at once for a biopsy. Instead, she asked, "Are you expecting your period soon?" I replied, "Yes, any day." She said. "Check your breasts again in a few days after your period has started. The lump will probably be gone. If not, call me again. But if it has disappeared, there is something you can do to prevent it from recurring." "What?" I asked enormously relieved. "Try eliminating all caffeine from your diet." Well, that sounded much too simple to be true. But I tried it. No more coffee for me. And wouldn't you know it, it worked! I haven't had painful breasts since I stopped drinking coffee.

If you are a regular coffee drinker, even if it's only two or three cups a day, suddenly cutting out caffeine can cause headaches. Usually they start about 12 to 24 hours after the last dose of caffeine and can be quite severe. Fortunately, the headache disappears after a day or two. It won't return unless caffeine is reintroduced on a regular basis and then withdrawn again. If you drink more than several cups of coffee, tea, or cola per day, you may prefer to reduce your intake slowly before cutting it out completely. Women who stop drinking coffee and other caffeinated drinks because of premenstrual symptoms should be aware that if a headache occurs it may very well be "caffeine withdrawal" and not a PMS symptom.

If you can't give up coffee or chocolate all month long, you'll find that even reducing your intake seems to help. Stay away from caffeine during the seven to ten days before your next period. That should alleviate much of the pain and discomfort.

Eliminating all caffeine may not be 100 percent effective for all women but it does help in many cases. In addition, reducing caffeine during the premenstrual period might also reduce the edginess and irritability often associated with PMS.

If, after several caffeine-free months, breast pain persists, you might want to check with your doctor about the several medical treatments available.

Some doctors recommend oral contraceptives or a low-dose hormone pill to keep your hormonal balance steady throughout the month. However, for some women with sensitivity to extra estrogen, this treatment may not prove acceptable.

A new drug, danazol (Danocrin), usually used to treat endometriosis, is sometimes prescribed for severe cases of fibrocystic breast disease. Danazol works by stopping ovulation, thereby preventing the production of progesterone, which causes breast tissue buildup. There are some side effects associated with danazol, but fewer than in most hormone treatments. Its major drawback is its fairly expensive price.

Some research has correlated higher prostaglandin production with the fibrous cysts, pain and tenderness. Several doctors who prescribed anti-prostaglandin medication found their patients were relieved of breast pain along with several other physical PMS symptoms.

Finally, surgery can be used in cases when cysts cause extreme pain or if cancer is suspected. In a simple procedure, the cysts are drained to remove the fluid. The fluid is then checked for the presence of cancerous cells. In 80 to 90 percent of cases these cysts are not malignant. Sometimes unusually painful or persistent nonmalignant cysts are removed from the breast.

Headaches

Many women have headaches in the days just before menstruation. Some experience migraines that seem to occur cyclically—only during PMS week. The start of menstrual flow usually brings an end to such headache pain.

Women often describe the premenstrual headache as a "steel vise around the forehead." Although in some months the pain might be dull and tolerable, in other months it can be throbbing, sharp, and continuous. Headaches associated with PMS seem to last longer and are more painful than headaches that occur at other times in the cycle.

If you have regular headaches, be sure to chart their occurrence on your PMS calendar. Some headaches are not related to the menstrual cycle and may be indicative of another problem, either physical or emotional.

Admittedly, many headaches, even premenstrual headaches, are caused by the emotions. Stress, conflict, unpleasant events can all lead to headaches and migraines. Some women who are also suffering other PMS symptoms may be less resilient and less able to cope with otherwise difficult situations.

But there are also physical causes of headaches. Although the origins of such pain remains much of a medical mystery, doctors now understand some of the physiological roots of premenstrual headaches.

Of all headaches, 90 percent are caused by the abnormal contraction or dilation of blood vessels in the brain. Hormonal changes may be responsible for some shifts in blood flow as well as other changes in the body that could contribute to headaches.

For example, fluid retention can account for some premenstrual headaches. As the brain membranes become swollen with water, headaches and migraines may result. Many doctors who treat women with PMS suggest a diet low in salt (which binds water to body cells, including brain cells). In some cases, a mild diuretic taken the week before menstruation may help.

Low blood sugar is also recognized as a contributing factor of many premenstrual headaches. Therefore, try to eat six small meals a day and keep from overindulging in sugars and carbohydrates, especially in the week or so before menstruation.

Some doctors feel that a deficiency in pyridoxine (vitamin B6) can cause headaches. Studies done in Australia and England have shown that 80 percent of women with premenstrual headaches found relief when they took vitamin B6 supplements. In addition, almost two-thirds of the women reported a lessening of their other PMS symptoms, notably depression and aggression. Vitamin B6 therapy will be discussed further in Chapter 8.

Often, the best and simplest cure for premenstrual headache is to take two aspirins and a nap. A little extra sleep can work wonders on a headache and may ease other PMS symptoms as well.

Some headaches, though, will not respond to simple treatment. Headaches that are rooted in chronic anxiety or depression usually need to be treated with prescriptive medicines as well as psychological therapy. Some women with headaches that last for days or weeks and recur frequently may need to seek such help.

A special note: Some doctors attribute all menstrually related headache pain to neurosis or the imagination. If your doctor seems to be placing you in this category, you may want to seek another physician. In addition, some doctors still prescribe tranquilizers regardless of the menstrual complaint. Unfortunately, tranquilizers are not effective in most premenstrual headaches and may worsen other symptoms. When used as a treatment for PMS tranquilizers should only be prescribed in certain cases involving anxiety.

Migraines are another form of premenstrual headache that often resist simple treatment. Migraines are distinguished from other headaches by certain visual disturbances (the migraine aura) that precede the pain, by a sensation of "pins and needles" or numbness prior to the pain, and intense pain that often occurs only on one side of the face or head.

Some doctors hold that migraines are hereditary. Others say there is a "migraine personality"—for example, a person who is something of a perfectionist. But whatever the reason, there is a biochemical correlation. Scientific tests have shown that people with migraines have a higher level of the chemical serotonin. Serotonin regulates the dilation and contraction of blood vessels.

Although it is not completely understood why women who have migraines often get them only during the premenstrual week, there are a few prescriptive drugs available that can prevent a migraine from occurring. One, propranolol hydrochloride (Inderal) is a vaso-constrictor. Another, methysergide maleate (Sansert), works to inhibit serotonin production. Both drugs are effective, but may cause several side effects. If you suffer from recurring severe migraines, check with your physician to see if either one is appropriate for you.

In general, if you suffer from premenstrual headaches or migraines there are a few things you can do, particularly during the week or so before your period, to prevent them or lessen their severity:

Emotions can cause a headache, so try to avoid stress. If you must face a stressful situation, try to maintain a relaxed state of mind, especially before your period.

Eat several small meals a day and maintain a sensible diet. It is known that many foods can trigger headache pain as well as migraines by expanding blood vessels in the brain. Stay away from anything smoked, pickled, fermented, or processed. Avoid alcoholic drinks, especially red wine. Other recognized causes of headaches include chocolate, monosodium glutamate (MSG), and cigarettes. Caffeine constricts blood vessels and might initiate a migraine. To avoid low blood sugar and the headaches that can result, never attempt to fast or skip meals during PMS time. Chapter 8 will list the foods to eat and those to avoid prior to your period.

Joint and Muscle Pain

Another common physical symptom of premenstrual syndrome is pain felt in the muscles or joints. Women with this symptom notice a stiffness or a dull ache in the shoulders, back, hips, knees, legs, ankles, or hands. Shoulder tension and backache seem to be the most frequent complaint. Some women who have rheumatism or arthritis suffer from flare-ups of these conditions just prior to menstruation or notice that attacks are most severe at that time.

Usually, the bouts with cyclical joint and muscle pain are not severe, but they occur often enough to cause a woman to feel achy and out-of-sorts. Being unable to accomplish everyday tasks with ease can understandably make a person feel irritable, clumsy, or slightly depressed.

Once menstrual flow begins, these symptoms disappear. If the aches and stiffness do not go away after your period starts, the pain may be symptomatic of another condition and you should consult your doctor.

There are several theories to account for the joint and muscle pain that occurs premenstrually. Some doctors feel much of it is due to tension. Emotional or mental tension causes muscles in the body to contract. Continual contraction over several hours or days can lead to stiffness and pain. Some simple exercises, particularly yoga stretches, may help the muscles to relax again. The causes of premenstrual tension will be explored more fully in the next chapter.

Other doctors feel that joint and muscle pain is due to increased production of prostaglandins during the premenstrual period. Several studies have shown there is an excess of prostaglandins in the joint fluid of arthritis patients. Furthermore, anti-prostaglandin medications seem to bring considerable relief to women with this particular PMS symptom. You can help yourself by taking aspirin or acetaminophen (Tylenol) during the premenstrual days. You might also want to try products such as Aspercreme, which can provide pinpoint relief for minor arthritic, rheumatic, back, and other muscle pain during the premenstrual period.

Finally, water and salt retention can cause swelling in the joints, which may lead to pain. Cutting down your salt intake during the ten to fourteen days before menstruation might give you some relief from premenstrual joint pain.

Clumsiness and Accidents

A good number of women are affected by clumsiness and lack of coordination during the premenstrual time. Accidents just seem to happen more frequently then.

Janice R., 35, a medical researcher, says,

> It's almost funny. I'll be washing the dishes or putting them away and suddenly a glass will just jump out of my hands. I must break a glass every month. But that's when I know I'm entering my premenstrual phase.

Many women drop things, bump into things, burn themselves while cooking, and cut themselves accidentally during the days before menstruation. Sometimes everything seems to go wrong as accidents and mistakes follow one after the other.

Some of the accidents and clumsiness can be attributed to physical causes. For example, muscle stiffness and joint swelling can interfere with normal coordination. Bouts with low blood sugar can also affect reflexes and reaction time.

Furthermore, the bodily aches and pains associated with PMS may detract from fully concentrating on the task at hand.

Emotional changes during the premenstrual days can also contribute to clumsiness and accidents. Lethargy, depression, feeling not quite yourself can result in slower reactions and diminished

129

concentration. Sometimes ordinary precautions are overlooked, ignored, or seem too troublesome to perform. Mood swings, irritability, and aggressiveness can also cause people to act impulsively and recklessly, increasing the chances for a mishap or accident.

But what is important to remember is that sometimes the accidents just *seem* to happen more frequently then. Because of the prevailing negative social attitudes concerning menstruation, women tend to blame accidents occurring premenstrually on their hormones. Indeed, many people have the impression that statistics prove more mishaps, even violence and crime, take place around the time of menstruation. In reality, such surveys are hard to come by and are hardly conclusive.

Alcohol and PMS

Some women find that an alcoholic drink or two helps to relieve some of their physical aches and pains during the premenstrual days. A glass of wine or a mixed drink can also soothe jangled nerves and help a person to relax. But other women turn to alcohol to blot out anxiety, tension, frustration, and depression. Some try to suppress their feelings of aggression, hostility, anger, and rage by drowning them with liquor.

In one survey, over two-thirds of women related their drinking to the days before menstruation. Counselors who work with alcoholics confirm the observation that women tend to abuse alcohol primarily during the premenstrual time.

Although research is limited, existing evidence strongly points to a relationship between the hormonal fluctuations of the menstrual cycle and a woman's ability to absorb and tolerate alcohol.

As stated earlier, a woman who may be able to handle several drinks at mid-cycle may notice she feels quite "high" or tipsy after only a drink or two just before her period.

Medical studies have shown that when given controlled amounts of alcohol, the highest blood alcohol levels are found in women who are premenstrual.

The decreased tolerance of alcohol may be directly linked to the drop in hormone levels that occurs prior to menstruation. In addition, since fluid retention is a marked feature of the premenstrual phase, alcohol is absorbed more quickly and efficiently into the bloodstream, thus carrying an increased effect.

Drinking interferes with the thinking process, reduces coordination, and dulls reflexes. If it is true that more women drink and drink more heavily during the premenstrual week, this could, in some measure, account for the increase in accidents during this time. It may also help explain the reported increases in crime, child abuse, and suicide attempts committed by women during the premenstruum.

In general, if you do enjoy moderate drinking, be aware of your monthly cycle. On the days when you are premenstrual, pay attention to your tolerance level and don't exceed it. This may mean having fewer drinks (but getting the same effect). Too much alcohol can produce depression and anxiety, which may increase other PMS symptoms and decrease your ability to cope.

Other Physical Symptoms

This chapter has attempted to explain the biological sources of the major physical symptoms of premenstrual syndrome—that is, those symptoms that are experienced most frequently by the majority of women with PMS. There remains a catalogue of other physical symptoms—some would say at least 40 more—that can occur during the premenstrual phase.

A good number of them, such as acne, "period pimples," boils, and styes, can be associated with the change in body chemistry in the second half of the menstrual cycle. Others can be related to periodic fluid/salt retention, low blood sugar, and the increased production of prostaglandins. For some women, the days before menstruation bring on an outbreak of a pre-existing condition, including herpes, asthma, and rheumatism.

It is important to recognize your symptoms, no matter how unique they may seem to be. Keep a record of when they occur to determine if they are related to your hormonal cycle.

Whatever your symptoms, you needn't suffer through them month after month, just because they appear only around the time of your period. Try various self-help methods. And if needed, your doctor may be able to prescribe medication or treatment for symptomatic relief.

Most women go through minor physical changes throughout the menstrual cycle. A few women experience these changes in a more marked and painful way. What is emerging is the fact that PMS is a highly individual phenomenon, yet the changes do happen to the majority of women. It's an old saying, but it may be true: "It's all part of being a woman."

But rather than rejecting our bodies and resisting these natural fluctuations, we should instead learn to accept ourselves and adapt to the premenstrual changes. At the heart of it, we should not be ashamed that our bodies are different from men's. Instead, we should celebrate that fact.

A great number of women today would do well to practice what our grandmothers did: before your period, use less salt, eat several small nutritious meals a day, stay away from too many harsh substances (alcohol, caffeine), and get plenty of rest. In other words, respect your womanliness enough to give yourself good premenstrual care.

Fortunately, today you can take control by understanding the foundations of the symptoms and doing what you can to alleviate your cyclical aches and pains yourself. Should you decide to see a doctor, you can use this knowledge to work with him or her to find a treatment that will put an end to your PMS symptoms.

6

YOUR MIND, MOODS, AND EMOTIONS

The Psychology of PMS

About once a month, I'd become a different person. I would yell, pick fights, become unbelievably aggressive. It terrifies me. I don't like to think that's the way I am. I'm a nice, quiet person the rest of the month. But the days before my period I feel like a monster.

Evelyn C., 38
Housewife

Premenstrual Emotions

The physical complaints associated with premenstrual syndrome may be difficult to bear, but for the woman who suffers from major psychological changes, the emotional effects of PMS are often much more disturbing and devastating.

If you have ever felt depressed, tired, tense, anxious, irritable, or hostile during your premenstrual days, you are not alone. At least half of all women who have premenstrual syndrome experience both bodily and emotional changes. In addition, some women suffer only from psychological symptoms.

Many women are alarmed and ashamed of their feelings during the premenstrual phase, especially if those feelings prompt them to act irrationally or violently. No matter what the emotional symptoms, women can feel confused and out of control. To add to this dilemma, women often punish themselves internally, torturing themselves for acts and emotions they see as unacceptable.

A woman might not connect her tension, crying spells, or hostility to her menstrual cycle. Therefore, if these feelings are happening to you, you should mark them on your menstrual chart. If your symptoms are related to PMS, they will occur after the time of ovulation and will disappear around the time of menstruation.

Sometimes, someone close to you may notice your periodic mood swings and connect them with your menstrual cycle before you do.

Your husband/partner/work associate might have said something like, "Is it getting close to your period? You always seem to cry/be irritable/become anxious before your period starts." When this subject is approached in a caring manner, it can help a woman to recognize her premenstrual pattern.

However, some men use this as a means to put down a woman's feelings, to say her emotions or her perceptions are not valid because of her menstrual cycle. This experience can be demeaning, demoralizing and depersonalizing. Geraldine D., 25, a cosmetics saleswoman agrees.

> My husband won't take me seriously if I am upset about something he said or did. He just shrugs it off, saying, "Uh, oh, it must be that time of the month again." It may be nowhere near that time of the month, but his saying it stings. He's telling me that my feelings don't really count because I'm a woman and have a menstrual cycle.

Yet we all know men go through occasional mood swings. Which secretary has not sometimes seen her boss act irrationally? Which wife has not coped when her husband became inexplicably moody? All men go through periods of anxiety, irritability, exhaustion, tension, and depression. But no one winks and says, "It must be his testosterone acting up again."

A man's emotions are taken seriously and are assumed to be caused by legitimate, non-body, non-hormonal reasons. Yet when a woman goes through the same feelings we say, "Oh, it must be her period" or "You know, women and their hormones."

It is time we realized that our *emotions are valid no matter what time of the month it is.* We should take our feelings seriously and try to deal with them, rather than sweeping them under a "PMS rug."

Hormones and biochemical changes may bring on feelings of sadness, depression, tension, and anxiety. But these feelings do not occur in an emotional vacuum. Instead they are probably a specific reaction to each individual's life circumstances. In some women, premenstrual changes simply intensify psychological states present all through the cycle.

So, in order to begin to understand and cope with those sometimes troubling and confusing premenstrual feelings, we need to *recognize* our emotions when they happen. Let's start by taking a look at the most common emotional changes women experience during the premenstrual phase.

Tension

If you have premenstrual tension, you know what it feels like. Usually it starts three to five days before your period. It creeps up slowly and may be punctuated by moments of panic, hours of savage self-criticism, entire days when the world seems bleak and hopeless. You may feel oddly unsettled, suffer from floating anxiety, find it difficult to concentrate. You may have an excruciating headache or painfully stiff muscles, especially in your neck and shoulders. Overall you feel gloomy, edgy, and not at all like yourself.

As the tension increases over the days, it becomes more and more difficult to control. Finally, you feel as if you are about to snap—and sometimes you do, snapping at co-workers and losing your temper around your loved ones. Premenstrual tension probably causes more interpersonal havoc and misunderstanding than any other symptoms of PMS.

Of all the emotional symptoms, tension is the most commonly reported by women with PMS. In fact, the entire syndrome was first described as premenstrual tension. It was called PMT until just recently when many other symptoms, not related to tension, were also attributed to the premenstruum.

What causes the tension? Unfortunately, there is no simple answer because there are both physical and psychological roots, and very often they are closely intertwined.

Water retention may be one leading source of premenstrual tension. Fluid and salt retention can cause changes in the way brain signals are sent, which may result in tension and anxiety. Physical bloating can also alter your mood and disposition.

The birth-control pill may be another cause. Tension, anxiety, and depression are recognized side effects of oral contraceptives. For some reason, these symptoms may persist even after the Pill is discontinued. (On the other hand, some women find their premenstrual symptoms eased by oral contraceptives. Physicians do not yet fully understand these paradoxical reactions.)

Another cause of premenstrual tension can be a strong wish to avoid pregnancy. If there is a chance of unwanted pregnancy or contraceptive failure, a woman might live in tense anticipation of the appearance of her monthly flow. Any delay in the start of her period (which is common enough) may lead to days of heightened anxiety.

Delayed menstruation or long intervals between periods is sometimes associated with increased severity of PMS symptoms. Since late or irregular periods may indicate anovulatory cycles (cycles without ovulation and therefore without progesterone) a few doctors have speculated that the lack of progesterone may be the underlying cause of PMS. Frequent late periods or continuously irregular menstrual cycles may point to a disturbance in the endocrine system or an imbalance of any one of the number of reproductive hormones making up this system. This theory may be substantiated by clinical observations that some women with severe PMS seem to have trouble conceiving.

The menstrual taboo, as described in Chapter 4, also plays a powerful role in the way a woman deals with the premenstrual time. Some researchers believe that premenstrual tension may be the result of unconscious inner conflicts concerning menarche and menstruation, sexuality, and being a woman.

Often, physical and psychological causes are meshed, the one blending into the other. For example, if a woman normally lives with a high level of tension, any additional physical or emotional premenstrual symptom may lead to an "overload." A woman who tends to be anxious, nervous, or run-down will probably be more affected by negative emotions during PMS time.

138

Some studies have shown that women with severe premenstrual tension tend to react poorly to stressful situations, are more prone to psychosomatic illness, and have higher neuroticism scores. PMS, then, exacerbates pre-existing emotional problems, rather than causing them.

In addition, continual work pressure, chronic financial difficulties, or enduring family troubles can also worsen premenstrual tension. Conversely, because of lowered self-image or other emotional changes, events sometimes seem much worse than they really are. It can help to try to keep things in perspective and to tell yourself that in a few days they'll get better. A woman with PMS should take outside circumstances into account and remember that it's "PMS time" before castigating herself and adding to her personal stress.

If the underlying cause is deeply seated emotional problems or if PMS is intensifying other life problems, those problems will have to be dealt with before premenstrual tension can be diminished.

Since some tension may be caused by physiological factors, you can begin overcoming PMS by controlling those elements. To start, try reducing premenstrual water retention by following the guidelines set in Chapter 5. Some doctors and nutritionists recommend supplements of vitamin B6, a common treatment of PMS, which will be further described in Chapter 8. In addition, a regular exercise routine can help, as well as getting sufficient sleep (which may mean extra rest during PMS time). In general, avoid stressful situations during PMS time. If you need to, rearrange your schedule so that your stress load is reduced. The last chapter will concentrate on how to live with PMS on a day-to-day basis.

Crying Spells

During the days before your period starts, you may find yourself constantly on the verge of tears. If you are like a good number of women, you might cry over what seem like the littlest, silliest things. Some women say they feel hypersensitive to criticism. The

least comment about their work, their appearance, whatever, ca
touch off a bout of depression or a flood of tears. A few women g
through periods of deep despair, self-pity, and/or self-persecutio

A number of factors that can cause crying spells come into pla
during the premenstrual time. Certainly, biological and hormona
factors have a role in influencing mood, although just how th
happens is not yet fully understood.

But personality and psychological factors are also importan
Life may not be going the way we had hoped. We may be dealin
with our lost dreams, our own shortcomings. Tears may also be
reaction to stress, a buildup of nerves, or increased premenstrua
anxiety. Some women who go through prolonged crying spel
may be expressing unmet personal needs or other buried psycho
logical problems. Anger, frustration, or a sense of powerlessne
can also come out in tears. These, too, must be taken into accou
when attempting to treat PMS.

Perhaps, as odd as it may seem, premenstrual crying spells ma
actually serve a purpose, and we should not be too quick to elim
nate them. We shouldn't think we are emotionally unstabl
because we are more sensitive and closer to tears during PMS tim
Psychologists have long noted that woman's greater ability to cr
may actually be a sign of mental health. Once a cycle, those tea
may serve the purpose of releasing inner tension or stress, wheth
it is biological or psychological in origin.

So, unless the crying spells are crippling, we would probably d
well to accept that part of our lives and use the experience to lear
about and strengthen ourselves.

Hostility

Some women report feeling excessively irritable during that tim
of the month. You may have uncontrollable fits of temper, or fee
unacceptably aggressive. You might feel like a time bomb ready t
explode. Right before your period, an ugly, black mood may de
scend upon you that doesn't lift until after menstruation ha
started.

There has been quite a bit of speculation that PMS causes violen behavior, but hormones in themselves cannot prompt those unpleasant, uncontrollable feelings of rage and hostility. Instead, several physiological factors may be at work here. For example, PMS often brings periodic bouts with low blood sugar, and low blood sugar may be related to increased irritability. Premenstrual water and salt retention can lead to greater tension, which may break out as an act of hostility. Excessive prostaglandin production has been associated with irritability. Of course, premenstrual aches and pains that last for days can understandably result in a nervous overload, a shorter fuse, a hostile reaction. As discussed in the previous chapter, some women turn to drinking during their premenstrual phase; it is well known that excessive alcohol consumption can ignite explosive behavior. Cyclical patterns of rage and violence may also be caused by a physical brain dysfunction such as "limbic rage" that can be triggered by premenstrual symptoms. All these factors must be taken into account when examining the source of premenstrual hostility.

But psychological factors must also be examined. Inappropriate bursts of rage often result when anger, hurts, and upsets have been bottled up inside. Frequently, a person may not know how to deal with those feelings when they happen. It is not uncommon for a woman to feel totally unable to express her anger, especially when the problem is compounded by the fear of losing her job, her husband, her lover. Sometimes, the fear is based on losing one's self-image. "I am a nice person. I can't believe I could have such overwhelming rage inside me. It frightens me to think I could have such feelings." A woman might have enormous shame attached to expressions of anger or aggressiveness. Nonetheless, if those feelings are there, they can only be suppressed, ignored, or rationalized for so long. Premenstrual changes may trigger an overload. The lid blows off, the time bomb explodes.

A woman's life situation must also be considered. She may have a troubling, unhappy background. There may be money problems, marriage troubles, conflicts with the children. She may suffer from profoundly personal problems. Add to these the biological changes prior to menstruation, changes she may resent and detest, and such a person might strike out as an act of frustration and desperation. If a woman feels powerless over her life and her body, she may turn to violence as a means of expression. Acts of violence are often attempts to regain or assert control over a situation or other people. (There is such a fear and loathing of violence in women, we need to be reminded that many men react violently when frustrated. In general, men are quicker to raise their voices, lose their temper, shout at or bully another person. Men are also more likely to push, shove, or hit to gain control or to get their own way. When it comes to criminal behavior, men are almost ten times as likely to act violently. Yet no one suggests that male biology or male hormones *cause* violence.)

If you have struck out and have physically hurt somebody during your premenstrual days, you may have been overwhelmed with remorse and regret afterward. Yet you shouldn't dismiss or ignore the episode just because it happened before your period. You will need to find the means within yourself to cope with your frustrations and irritability *without* resorting to violence. It may be helpful to seek counseling to prevent future attacks. If you are hurting your children, call a child-abuse hot line or a Parents Anonymous group. You will not be judged, but you will receive immediate help.

Most women, however, have never actually committed an act of violence during their premenstrual phase and never will—they only *feel* like it. You may have thought to yourself, "I felt like killing him!" or "I wanted to strangle her!" Be assured, there is a great difference between *thinking* about something and actually *doing* it. There is simply no medical evidence to indicate that hormones can compel a person to do something against her own will. This is important to any woman who feels she may be losing self-control to "overpowering forces" within her.

Depression

Women who experience premenstrual depression often say this is the worst symptom. It is potentially the most serious.

Sometimes the depression may be mild. You might feel slightly "down," you might be close to tears all day long, you might believe that nothing you do is right. Other times there may be extended periods of crying spells, diminished alertness, and episodes of harsh self-criticism. Occasionally, premenstrual depression can deepen to the point where the self seems worthless, the world meaningless, the future hopeless—and there may be thoughts of suicide.

Numerous studies have attempted to correlate anxiety, depression, and suicide to the premenstrual phase, but the results remain conflicting. It is admittedly very difficult to measure accurately such subjective and transitory moods as sadness, hopelessness, and despair. Although it appears that psychiatric admissions, suicide attempts, and criminal behavior occur more frequently during the premenstrual week, it is also known that a personal crisis or an extremely strong emotion can cause a change in the uterine lining, initiating menstrual bleeding. Therefore, it is almost impossible to separate cause and effect.

It is doubtful that PMS drives women to suicide, but it probably can worsen a pre-existing condition. Extreme emotional problems or the inability to deal with difficult life circumstances can cause depression; PMS merely adds to the difficulties.

Problems related to pregnancy may also bring on despondency. For example, for a woman who desperately wishes to conceive but is unable to, the body's premenstrual symptoms signal failure once again. As her menstrual period approaches, she may feel increasingly gloomy until her period is over and there is once again hope for the new cycle. In another woman, there may be a longing for a child or additional children, a wish that may be impossible to fulfill for whatever reason; the approaching period is a reminder that the wish cannot come true. Finally, if a woman has had an abortion, the premenstrual time may stir up unpleasant memories about the circumstances of the abortion or ambivalent feelings about her decision to terminate the pregnancy.

The emotional roots of premenstrual depression can go very deep indeed. They are also profoundly personal and individual, and must be taken into account before any kind of appropriate treatment can be recommended.

Having explored some of the emotional causes, we must also consider physical reasons for premenstrual depression.

Various drugs and medications can produce depression, including oral contraceptives and other synthetic or natural hormonal treatments. Long-term use of mood-altering drugs and excessive consumption of alcohol can also cause chronic depression, which may worsen during the premenstrual days. Therefore, if you are suffering from depression, it would be wise to consider everything you are taking. Discontinuing those drugs may lift the depression. You might wish to consult with your doctor.

Water retention can also lead to depression. It is thought that changes in water/salt/potassium levels can lead to chemical changes in the nervous system, possibly producing a depressed mood.

The lack of vitamin B6 has been correlated to a variety of mood disorders, including depression. Although scientific evidence is far from complete, vitamin supplements may help some women with premenstrual depression.

In the meantime, what should you do if you feel gloomy and disheartened during your premenstrual days? If your depressions are mild to moderate, you can probably find relief through counseling, whether private or group. Just talking about it can help. Use your feelings to analyze your life situation. You may find a way to change or improve a situation that may be underlying your low spirits. Finally, it can help to remember that the depression is temporary and will lift once your period starts.

If your depression is deep, however, you may need medication (possibly anti-depressants), and that involves medical help. Your doctor may be able to refer you to a specialist who can provide you with appropriate treatment.

If you are deeply depressed or are thinking of suicide, you should seek help immediately. Telephone a suicide prevention hot line, or go to the nearest emergency ward of a hospital. You will receive help. Do not ignore your feelings just because they happen during PMS time.

Too often, though, doctors prescribe tranquilizers to women who complain of menstrually related depression. Unfortunately, tranquilizers and other sedatives *do not* work for premenstrual depression and can worsen it. If this is all your doctor can suggest for you, you should seek another physician who may prescribe vitamin B6 therapy, antidepressant medication, or other appropriate prescription treatments. If searching for a new doctor seems too overwhelming while you are depressed, wait until after your period has started and your depression has lifted. Then find a doctor who has a greater understanding of PMS symptoms.

Fatigue

Fatigue, lethargy, increased tiredness, or just a heavy, dull feeling are very common during the premenstrual week. Some mornings it's harder to pull yourself out of bed, you feel sluggish at work, daily routines seem like too much effort; you might want to do nothing more than crawl back to bed and pull the covers over your head.

This can be a puzzling symptom, especially if you are normally active and energetic. You might be surprised that you seem to crave extra sleep several days before your period starts.

Fatigue can be brought on by low blood-sugar levels. Extra water retention, which leads to bloating, may also make you feel lethargic.

Certain drugs or medications, such as tranquilizers, might also cause sleepiness or lethargy. The Pill may also lead to fatigue in some women. If you are taking diuretics, they can cause a drop in potassium, resulting in lethargy. Of course, drinking alcoholic beverages the evening before may make you feel extra tired the next day, especially during PMS time.

Some doctors theorize that high levels of estrogen and progesterone may account for premenstrual lethargy. In particular, excess progesterone seems to foster fatigue.

Fatigue and lethargy may also be due to psychological factors. For example, premenstrual depression or tension can lead to increased exhaustion. If you are also coping with stressful situations at work or at home, the addition of other PMS symptoms may result in an extra need for sleep.

Not all fatigue is directly related to PMS; therefore if you feel that you suffer from *extreme* fatigue, you should receive a thorough physical checkup. Even if your exhaustion occurs cyclically, it may be due to a deficient red-cell blood count, slow thyroid function, or a malfunction of the nervous system.

In general though, unless there is a diagnosed condition, prescriptive medicines do not seem to help this PMS symptom. Fortunately, there is a great deal *you* can do to increase your premenstrual energy level.

Try changing your eating habits during your premenstrual days to include more protein. Lean meats, fish, dairy products, eggs, and unsalted nuts are good sources of protein. In addition, eat five or six small meals a day.

That may seem sensible enough, but if you are like most people, when listlessness sets in you might want to reach for a chocolate bar or a nice, sticky pastry. Sweets and carbohydrates can give you an energy rush, but it will probably be followed by a greater drop in your blood-sugar level and you'll feel even more listless than before. In order to avoid fatigue, it's important to keep blood-sugar levels on an even keel during PMS time.

A regular routine of exercise can also keep premenstrual fatigue at a minimum. Physically active women seem to have less problem with this sympton than do other women. Beginning an exercise program might seem too exhausting to even think about during PMS week. If so, start after your cycle begins again and keep it up throughout the month. You might be surprised how much better you feel next time around.

In addition, since some doctors think low levels of vitamin B6 may lead to fatigue and other PMS symptoms, supplementary vitamins may help to overcome premenstrual exhaustion.

If you experience periodic fatigue, try to pace yourself during those days. By becoming familiar with your cycle, you can plan your daily schedule to reduce outside pressures. Women may also need a bit more sleep or rest during the premenstrual days. Taking a short daily nap or going to bed an hour early the week before your period may help to moderate fatigue.

Anxiety

Several studies have shown that anxiety levels in women seem to be significantly higher during the premenstrual phase.

If you suffer from heightened anxiety in the days before your period, you'll probably recognize this symptom. Usually there is a vague sense of panic, maybe even a little paranoia. Your stomach feels tight, your nerves are easily frazzled. You may feel agitated or have a tingling tremor that seems to signify something is about to go wrong.

Anxiety can also produce a host of physical symptoms, from stomach upsets to abdominal cramps, to diarrhea, to heart palpitations, to tension headaches prior to the onset of menstruation. Premenstrual anxiety can also worsen other PMS symptoms. High levels of anxiety can disrupt hormonal balances, which in turn may be the cause of various PMS symptoms. It is well known that anxiety can delay the start of menstruation (as well as bring it on). A delayed period is frequently associated with more severe PMS symptoms.

Denise D., 35, a tax lawyer, comments,

> *I seem to have a much rougher PMS time when my period is late. Each day just increases the misery, until I feel I can barely stand it.*

In general, anxiety works against you by increasing the number and severity of the symptoms while decreasing your natural ability to cope with them.

Unlike other PMS symptoms, there appears to be no known physical cause for premenstrual anxiety. (We must leave open the possibility that some biochemical source will be uncovered in the future.) However, personality factors are known to be very important. If a woman tends to be nervous, shy, inhibited, if she is a worrier, or if she places high expectations on herself and is overly self-conscious, she will probably fall victim to premenstrual anxiety and its many accompanying symptoms.

As in any emotional symptom of PMS, a woman (or her physician) must also take into account certain life factors such as a recent death in the family, divorce, and other problems at home or work.

In some cases, PMS is neither biological nor hormonal in its cause, but is psychogenic. For some women, anxiety underlies their psychological PMS symptoms, including tension, crying spells, depression, and the inability to handle frustration and irritability as well as the various physical symptoms. However, this is not meant to dismiss or denigrate the suffering of individual women whose symptoms are psychogenic.

In treating PMS, tranquilizers seem to help in those cases where the symptoms stem from anxiety. (As mentioned earlier, tranquilizers do not solve the problem for many women because anxiety is not their central problem.) However effective tranquilizers may be, they cannot eliminate underlying personality or emotional problems. If tranquilizers are prescribed for psychosomatic premenstrual syndrome, treatment should include appropriate counseling or psychological therapy.

Altered Sex Drive

Many women feel increased sexual desire during the days before menstruation begins. You may have noticed a greater interest in sex, that you seem to be more easily aroused during that time. You become excited more quickly and orgasms may seem stronger or more fulfilling.

Most researchers who have studied women's sexuality report that the vast majority of women do indeed experience a sexual peak prior to the onset of menstruation. (Well, at last we are coming to a positive premenstrual symptom!)

Scientific studies performed by Masters and Johnson concur. They have observed that during the luteal phase, or the second half of the menstrual cycle, women most easily reach the plateau phase of sexual excitement. In another study, Kinsey found that women who may masturbate only occasionally tend to do so during the premenstrual days.

In chapter 3, we learned how certain premenstrual changes

including water retention, can cause swelling in the sexual organs. The increased pressure may then be felt as heightened desire for sexual activity and the release of the pressure through orgasm.

Orgasm can also greatly relieve tension throughout the body, easing many physical PMS symptoms. Sexual contact can relieve many emotional symptoms as well. Anxiety, depression, and crying spells can be soothed by affection and tenderness. Just feeling the warmth and touch of the person you love can work wonders on the premenstrual blues. Close loving human contact can also calm jangled nerves and restore your sense of well-being.

If you do not have a steady sexual partner, or if you feel too irritable or edgy to be in intimate contact with another person, you can choose to masturbate in order to relieve sexual tension. There is no reason to feel ashamed or guilty about masturbation. It is now known to be a normal facet of human sexuality.

Some women, however, do not feel increased sexual desire during the premenstruum. In fact they feel just the opposite—that they could not endure sexual contact at that time. Indeed, extreme tension, irritability, self-pity, and depression can extinguish any spark of sexuality.

For a few women, genital and breast swelling may cause pain instead of heightened pleasure. Certain drugs and medications can also dampen sexual response. The birth-control pill has this effect in some women, as does progesterone treatment. In fact, the Pill and progesterone seem to lessen sexual desire in some women throughout the menstrual cycle.

But for other women, normal increased sexual desire produces feelings of guilt, anxiety, and inhibition. They may be troubled by their feelings of sexual urgency, which may be thought of as wrong or unacceptable. If there are inner conflicts about sex and the body, premenstrual physical changes can cause them to surface.

PMS's Positive Side

Up till just this past section, the premenstrual phase looked pretty grim: aches and pains and tears and depression. But PMS also has a positive side.

We have already discussed increased sexual desire, which is seen as a premenstrual bonus for many women. A good number of us also have noted bursts of extra energy, elevated moods, vivid dreams, and enhanced creativity.

> *I feel very assertive, very good about myself during the time before my period. I know that the extra energy I have and that feeling of self-confidence reflects in my work. I get twice as much accomplished those days.*
>
> Barbara S., 31,
> Saleswoman.

Another woman, Sarah J., also 31, a physical therapist, bakes bread before her period.

> *I don't know what it is, but I'll wake up one morning with an urge to bake bread. I can hardly wait to get home from work and start mixing the flour, kneading the dough, smelling the yeast. It's almost sensual and very satisfying. Maybe it's the earth-mother in me coming out. I don't know. But I do enjoy my premenstrual time.*

A good number of women agree they feel more "domestic" before their period. They do extra cooking, baking, or cleaning the house. It can be a time of putting things in order.

Still other women feel more creative premenstrually. They write poetry, take out the easel and paint, pick up a needlework project, think of new ways to decorate their home.

Sometimes the premenstrual phase is a time of self-reflection, of "inner housekeeping." It can be a very important period of personal review and self-exploration. For some, it is a time of centering oneself, of accepting one's humanity and womanliness.

> *I have heard that many women cry before their period. Well, I do, too. Sometimes I'll cry at the drop of a hat, but it's a good crying. I'll be watching something tender on TV or my children will do something dear, and my eyes fill up. My heart is flooded with feelings of love for them*

> *or for my husband, for the world, for humanity, all the*
> *joy and all the suffering. Sometimes I could just cry and*
> *cry. But it strengthens me. It makes me feel a part of the*
> *earth, of the life-giving force.*

Ronnie L., who feels like this every cycle, is 35 and an executive secretary.

There must be many women who feel full of tenderness, who have increased compassion, who donate time to charity, who bake cookies for their children, who gladly clean the house, who achieve professional success during their premenstrual phase.

We don't know much about this positive side of PMS. After all, women who have these "symptoms" are not likely to seek medical help or report these feelings to a doctor. These women are also less likely to fill out questionnaires or participate in studies concerning PMS. Furthermore, questions about PMS focus on the negative symptoms. Therefore, knowledge about the entire spectrum of premenstrual experiences is biased toward the negative.

Physicians and scientists who are conducting research on the premenstrual syndrome should put effort into studying why some women have increased energy, greater creativity, and a general sense of well-being before menstruation. Perhaps by better understanding this facet, better solutions can be offered for premenstrual problems.

As in the physical symptoms of premenstrual syndrome, each woman experiences emotional symptoms in a unique and individual way. Probably no two women have exactly the same premenstrual emotional pattern. And if you are like most women, you'll notice variations in your symptoms from cycle to cycle and from year to year.

There have been efforts to correlate various biochemical mechanisms with premenstrual moods. Poor diet, vitamin and mineral deficiencies, lack of exercise, and other general health factors have also been implicated in producing premenstrual emotional symptoms. Although there has been progress in understanding the influence of physiological changes on our moods, we cannot assume that they alone cause them.

In the quest for a physical cause for PMS emotions, many psychological factors have been overlooked. To summarize, they include external stress, unresolved internal conflicts, relationship problems, conflicts about femininity, society's negative attitude toward the menstrual process, and sexual repression.

Premenstrual problems may also be a learned response (a high-symptom mother), and there may be heredity factors.

In a few cases, PMS might be used consciously or unconsciously as a way to manipulate others or to excuse unacceptable behavior. Some women rely on the "sick role" to control their environment, and still others wish to abdicate control over their lives. Hormones are used as a rationalization to avoid facing difficult issues or accepting responsibility for one's life.

Even though attempts have been made to ascribe certain personality types to women who experience emotional changes, no one stereotypical description emerges. There are too many individual differences. So, in spite of a multitude of theories and treatments, there is still no one effective solution to premenstrual emotional problems. PMS is a complex tapestry woven with biological, psychological, and sociological threads. It's hardly a wonder that the "cure" remains elusive. Through continued research and understanding, better approaches may be found.

In the meantime you can gain some reassurance that your feelings are real and that you are not imagining them. Premenstrual mood changes are not abnormal. Most women go through them. You're certainly not alone.

Try not to feel guilty or ashamed about the emotions that you experience during your premenstrual days.

Sadly, too many women try to "split" their personality, thinking "this is not me" for a week or so every cycle. Refusing to respect an emotion just because it is associated with your menstrual cycle is a way of denying an integral part of your self, of your being.

As women, we need to stop fighting and resisting our bodies and our feelings. Our feelings, throughout the month, are an essential part of us. They make up the full sphere of our humanity and womanliness.

7

"THOSE RAGING HORMONES"

The Sociology of Premenstrual Syndrome

I'm a basket case before my period starts. I can't do anything right in the office. I burst into tears at nothing, and I'm so irritable I feel like killing anyone who crosses my path. Some days I worry whether I might murder someone just before my period like those two women in England.

Geraldine D., 35
Department store
assistant buyer

Pandora's Box

There was a time when many of the world's problems were blamed on the menstrual period—blighted crops, diseased cattle, spoilt milk, turned wine. Although some myths remain, today we know there is no scientific, medical basis for thinking a menstruating woman is a danger to civilized society.

People are now beginning to believe that the *pre*menstrual woman is a hazard to herself and others. Employee absenteeism, industrial accidents, domestic violence, child abuse, manslaughter, murder, and suicide are all attributed to PMS. It's like Pandora's box—once the PMS lid is off, out fly the ills of the world.

The impression that women with PMS are totally out of control once a month has been reinforced by fiction and nonfiction books, magazine and newspaper articles, and television programs, which have featured hair-raising accounts of bizarre behavior by women in the throes of premenstrual syndrome.

At first, this view seems to be supported by recent medical evidence that shows physical, hormonal, and biochemical changes occurring in the female body prior to menstruation. It is easy to quickly conclude cause and effect: biological events *compel* women to behave in certain ways.

The confirmed existence of PMS poses many troubling questions. It's a feminist's nightmare.

Does PMS cause lowered work performance, decreased job efficiency, and poorer professional judgments? Will proof of PMS be used to discriminate against women in the job market? Will women be kept out of responsible positions? Will PMS be used against women in divorce cases and child-custody battles? Could PMS be used as an excuse for violence against women? ("My wife has PMS, officer, and once a month she goes crazy. This is the only way I can control her." "Your honor, she had PMS and attacked me. I killed her in self-defense.")

Does PMS mean women become so distraught during a cycle that they cannot be trusted to respond with reason to stressful situations? Does it mean that for a week or two every month women lose control over their bodies, their emotions, their behavior? Does it mean that "those raging hormones" compel women to commit acts of violence?

In short, are women controlled by their hormones? The core of the controversy surrounding premenstrual syndrome lies in this question.

It is tempting to evade the controversy by denying altogether the role hormones play in mood and psychobiology, as some feminists have vehemently argued. Another easy way to skirt the issue is to conclude, "Well, only a few women with really bad cases of PMS are controlled by their hormones. That shouldn't mean all of us are."

Unfortunately, we must still contend with the prevailing judgment that what is true for one woman is true for all women. A particular male boss, for example, may be a terrible employer, and people will say, "Well, he is a terrible boss." But if a particular female boss is dreadful to work for, people think, "Women make lousy bosses." Therefore, if it is popularly believed that a premenstrual woman cannot exercise self-control over her actions, and if a woman herself denies responsibility for her behavior during that time of the month (as some have, publicly on television and privately at home), the thinking goes that this, then, must be the case with all women.

For this reason, women should be concerned about the implications PMS may have for our lives. Already PMS has been called a "backlash against feminism" and the "male chauvinists' revenge."

Let's explore some of the controversy surrounding PMS, including the social and cultural influences on PMS, how PMS affects performance, and the role of hormones in behavior, particularly violent behavior.

Social Expectations and Premenstrual Syndrome

Although PMS has its basis in hormonal and biochemical changes, how a woman responds to premenstrual changes is also influenced by cultural expectations and social factors (including the menstrual taboo), as well as her upbringing, her education, and her relationships with other women, particularly her mother and other close female relatives.

Mothers and PMS

Several researchers have observed that high-symptom women more often than not have mothers who experienced severe premenstrual symptoms. It is unknown to what extent this is due to heredity or to learned behavior. Some researchers theorize that if a girl grows up observing her mother having a difficult time with various aspects of the menstrual cycle, the girl may expect to experience the same and react accordingly.

Education and PMS

If the basic facts about menstruation are not properly and positively presented by the mother, a young woman in this society has virtually no opportunities to learn about the menstrual cycle elsewhere. Health or sex education classes in public schools that deal with the experience of menstruation are usually brief and embarrassing, or glossy and superficial, or both. (Frequently girls are only shown a short film with cartoon characters—hardly the basis for sound knowledge about and respect for one's body and self.)

157

But if education about menstruation is scant, education about premenstrual syndrome is nonexistent. A teenager has no idea what to expect in the way of physical or emotional changes prior to her period. So as a young woman grows into adulthood, she has no understanding of what is happening to her body and her moods. The signals of change seem to be mysterious, confusing, and unpredictable. She begins to mistrust her body and loses confidence in her self.

Some gynecologists have called for increased knowledge about premenstrual syndrome through public health education programs. All women should know what it is and how to cope with it. (The next three chapters of this book offer help in coping with PMS symptoms.)

Religion and PMS

Sociologist Dr. Karen Paige of the University of California has surveyed the effects of religious upbringing on the severity of premenstrual symptoms. Her study indicated that the women who suffered most were those brought up as Roman Catholics and, second, those raised as Orthodox Jews. Protestant women seem to have fewer problems with PMS (although there are some variations because of the differences in sects). She postulates that the more traditional faiths are more restrictive and repressive to women, and the taboos against menstruation are more strictly enforced. Protestants, by the nature of their religious beliefs, are generally less dogmatic, more open to the improvement in women's status, and more tolerant of sexual and reproductive knowledge.

Interestingly, Dr. Paige also noted that women who adhered to and accepted the traditional concept of woman's role had greater problems with premenstrual syndrome. Therefore it would seem that upbringing is important to the way a woman perceives and handles her premenstrual phase.

Self-reports and PMS

Dr. Diane Ruble, Associate Professor of Psychology at New York University, suggests that reports by women of their premenstrual symptoms may be inflated due to learned expectations about the menstrual cycle. Dr. Ruble devised an experiment in which volunteers were told that through new scientific techniques involving an electroencephalogram, it was now possible to predict the expected date of the start of menstruation. (In fact, EEG patterns cannot predict menstruation.) The participants were connected by electrodes to a simulated EEG machine. The experimenter than pretended to read the results.

One group of women were informed they were premenstrual and their period should start in a day or two. A second group were told they were "intermenstrual." A third group was given no information at all and served as the control group for the experiment. The women were placed in their groupings at random.

Afterward, each woman answered a questionnaire concerning menstrual distress symptoms. The women who were falsely led to believe they were premenstrual reported higher incidences of PMS symptoms, including water retention and pain.

Dr. Ruble interpreted these results as supporting other research concerning the importance of psychosocial factors about the menstrual cycle. It appears that cultural expectations or learned beliefs can influence a woman's self-perception and lead her to overstate or exaggerate her cyclical changes.

This may also be true of women reporting bizarre or violent premenstrual behavior. For example, Christine M., 33, who was interviewed for this book, said that during her last argument with her husband, which occurred two days before her period started, she "picked up furniture and threw it across the room." Upon further questioning, she was asked to clarify the circumstances—that is, did she actually lift up a piece of furniture and project it some distance across the room? Christine replied, "No. I was trying to make my point, and I hit the back of a chair for emphasis and the chair fell over."

Women might exaggerate an experience, either bodily or behavioral, owing to cultural conditioning or learned associations about the premenstrual phase. In general, self-reports tend to conform to what is socially expected, according to Dr. Barbara Sommer, of the Department of Psychology at the University of California. She states that the social expectation is that women are "debilitated" and "out of control" during the time around menstruation. Those attitudes are communicated in subtle (and not-so-subtle) ways. Women internalize society's negative attitudes toward the menstrual process and "edit" their experiences, their self-perception, and even their self-esteem to fit the image of the archetypal woman ruled by the tides of her hormones.

PMS and Performance

Although there is relatively little scientific data concerning the way women experience their menstrual cycles over a lifetime, there is a virtual cornucopia of studies that have attempted to demonstrate the effects of the menstrual cycle on performance.

Tens of thousands of women have been tested at every point of the cycle. These women have included housewives, business women, college students, office workers, and factory employees. The studies have tested the ability to reason, to do arithmetic, auditory sensitivity, critical thinking, cognitive-task performance, complex problem solving, fitting concepts to data, higher-level intellectual performance, judgment making, mechanical comprehension, memory, olfactory sensitivity, perceptual motor tasks, perceptual speed, skin response, ability to spell, time estimation, verbal fluency, plus a long list of other standardized cognitive tasks and perceptual motor functions.

If you were expecting a distinct premenstrual dip, you would be mistaken.

The overwhelming majority of these studies show that there are *no fluctuations in a woman's performance in relation to her menstrual cycle*. The results of most tests simply do not lead to the conclusion that performance is adversely affected by the menstrual cycle. In fact, several independent researchers have shown that in arithmetic calculations, women performed with optimum accuracy during the premenstrual phase and that when given "insolvable puzzle" tests, women showed greater persistence premenstrually. It also appears that visual sensitivity and pattern discrimination peak during the premenstrual phase.

The few tests that did show some menstrual related variations were inconsistent, inconclusive, and self-contradictory, or were contradicted by other studies. Furthermore, studies that indicated premenstrual impairment tended to overstate the drop in performance in order to conform to the researcher's hypothesis. The summaries of those studies ignored the percentage of women who did *better* during PMS time as well as the majority of women who had no change.

But the great preponderance of tests show again and again that the menstrual cycle has no effect on performance.

This is certainly good news for all women, especially those of us who worry we're not doing as well during the premenstrual phase.

Paradoxically, women often believe they have diminished concentration, more difficulty in making critical judgments, and slower reaction time premenstrually. Other women believe that their athletic and/or mental performance is impaired before menstruation.

What we have is a gap between *perceived* ability and *actual* performance. For reasons having to do with cultural and social attitudes and expectations, many women (and men) honestly think PMS can decrease performance. The Tampax Corporation confirmed this in its report published in 1981: 35 percent of Americans believe the menstrual cycle affects a woman's ability to think, and 26 percent believe women can't function as well during that time of the month. These beliefs are reinforced by a woman's self-doubt about her body and her lack of confidence in her own ability to cope with premenstrual changes.

Yet even when women genuinely believe they are impaired premenstrually, when tested they do as well as women who believe the menstrual cycle has no effect on performance. Interestingly, a few tests have indicated that high-symptom women actually do better than low symptom women. In addition, women who are aware of their premenstrual feelings tend to do better on a variety of intellectual and cognitive tests than women who are not aware of their menstrual cycle.

These surprising results may be due to "trying harder"—in other words, the premenstrual woman is compensating for what she *perceives* to be a disadvantageous condition.

Dr. Sharon Golub, of the Department of Psychology at the

College of New Rochelle, stresses a point that is most important: "Although women may *think* they are impaired and less able to function, they are in fact not impaired and perform as well when premenstrual as at other times of the month."

PMS and Behavior

It's an age-old question: Do the female hormones control a woman's behavior?

Freud said "biology is destiny." Indeed, women's "inherent weakness" has been attributed to hormonal fluctuations for as far back in history as there are written records. Even in today's world, books have been written linking "those raging hormones" to everything from moodiness to madness to murder.

But the notions concerning the causes of behavior are based on a fundamental misconception about the relationship between hormones and behavior and the distinction between mood and behavior.

The interrelationship between hormones and mood is exceedingly complex—science still does not know precisely how and to what extent any one hormone affects mood. Furthermore, the higher centers of the brain, located in the cerebral cortex, which control thinking, reasoning, judgment, and other complex motor perceptual and cognitive functions, do not even have specific receptors for the sexual hormones and therefore the influence of estrogen and progesterone (and testosterone for that matter) is only indirect, if anything.

Because human beings are infinitely complicated, there can be no simple biological explanation for behavior. One or two hormones that may be high or low at any given point could not be the sole reason for outward actions. Instead, behavior is the result of the intricate interweaving of countless factors, including genetics, hormones, biochemical interreactions, environment, nutrition, general health, parental influences, personality, psychological factors, cultural expectations, role modeling, immediate circumstances, motivation, and individual will.

The distinct differences between mood and behavior are often blurred in a discussion involving PMS. For instance, we often don't feel like doing things (mood) that we do anyway (behavior) and vice versa.

For example, during PMS week, a woman might be depressed, irritable, and want nothing more than to stay home in bed all day (mood). Instead, she pulls off the covers, endures an hour of traveling to work on a crowded bus, and puts in a full, productive day on the job (behavior).

Conversely, a woman during the premenstrual phase may feel an irresistible urge to finish an entire container of chocolate chocolate-chip ice cream (mood), but she resists, knowing too much sugar would not be good for her before her period, and eats a wedge of low-salt cheese instead (behavior).

Many women feel convinced they will be impaired in a stressful situation during PMS time (mood), whereas in reality they do perfectly well on difficult intellectual tasks and cognitive test performances (behavior).

A good number of women with severe bouts of premenstrual tension or irritability say they fear hurting their baby, hitting their husband, killing someone (mood), yet they *don't* (behavior). This is a vital distinction: a woman with PMS may feel like doing something irrational or violent, but the vast majority control their urges and impulses and do not act on them.

It is an error to link all bizarre or violent behavior to PMS. After all, most violent acts are committed by men, and men, presumably, don't have PMS. Millions of women have extremely severe symptoms of PMS, yet they don't act out violently. If they did, every month countless people would suffer property damage, personal injury, and even death in a rampage of premenstrual women. Obviously, this is not the case. Only a tiny fraction of a percent of women do behave violently during the premenstrual phase, and we must vigorously question other factors (psychological, circumstantial, motivational, etc.) before attributing such actions solely to PMS.

Furthermore, most cases concerning violent behavior are based only on evidence of self-reporting. As already discussed, self-reports may be exaggerated and may not accurately indicate the exact phase of the menstrual cycle. Very few women involved in violent behavior are actually given medical tests (vaginal cytology, cervical mucus, measurement of hormones from the pituitary and the ovaries) to determine whether they were truly premenstrual at the time. Therefore, no clear relationship can be established between PMS and violent behavior.

In conclusion, hormonal fluctuations may *influence mood*, but they do not *control behavior*. Although PMS has its basis in hormonal and biochemical changes, premenstrual behavior is highly subject to psychological and sociological factors. *We* control our behavior, not the moon, or the tides, or our hormones.

PMS and Crime

Numerous attempts have been made to correlate the menstrual cycle to bizarre behavior, violent outbreaks, and criminal activity. Every now and again, statistics are published showing that 50, 60, or 70 percent of crimes committed by women take place during the premenstruum. Last year in England, when two women were charged with murder, PMS was used as the mitigating circumstance. In this country, PMS was introduced for the first time as a defense in a case involving child abuse.

These and other stories are what make the headlines; these are the women who are the subjects of television talk shows and magazine interviews. Much of what the general public knows about PMS is based on these sensational accounts.

What is the reality behind the statistics, the scary headlines? Is it true that all women are potential criminals during that time of the month? Do the female hormones, those raging hormones, promote violence if left unchecked?

Let's first take a look at those statistics. Depending on what survey is used, anywhere from half to three-quarters of female crime is said to take place during the premenstrual phase. The simple explanation seems to be that PMS causes criminal activity in women.

There are numerous problems associated with that conclusion.

1) The surveys do not clearly define the "premenstrual phase" or are not consistent in their definitions. One set of statistics may mean "the time from ovulation to the start of menstrual flow," which is about two weeks. (If 50 percent of crimes occur in two out of four weeks in the month, then the menstrual cycle obviously has no effect on criminal behavior.) Other surveys may place the premenstrual phase at three days, one week, or ten days before menstruation. Furthermore, the research methods used have been widely criticized as being inadequate and faulty. As a result, we just can't take these studies at face value. A closer examination should be made of the statistics before jumping to conclusions.

2) Most of the statistics are based on the self-reports of the apprehended woman. She may not know accurately what phase she is in. It is almost impossible to predict with certainty on what day one's period will start. There is also the possibility that a convicted woman will misrepresent the time she expects her period in order to gain court sympathy or to excuse her behavior. It is extremely rare for an arrested woman to be medically tested to determine the precise stage of her menstrual cycle.

3) Extreme stress can bring on the menstrual period. Committing a violent crime, getting caught, being arrested and detained in prison are extremely stressful situations, which can cause menstrual bleeding. The convicted woman or others might then look back and conclude, "Oh, she was premenstrual when she committed the crime because the next day her period started." It's a conundrum—did her period cause the crime, or did the crime cause her period?

4) Some experts feel that women who commit crimes do so throughout the cycle, but only get caught when they are premenstrual. They attribute this to lowered confidence, water retention, which might produce clumsiness or "lead legs," and low blood sugar, which can produce confusion or delayed reaction—all of which may prevent a criminal from getting away.

Therefore the statistics concerning PMS and crime will have to be more rigorously documented before any correlation can be established. As of now, the connection is tenuous.

165

With the preceding in mind, let's take a look at the three notorious criminal cases involving PMS.

There is a misconception in this country about the two murders in England—that PMS was used as a defense and that the two women were found "innocent" or were "acquitted" of their crimes. In actuality, both women were *convicted*. One woman pleaded guilty, the other was found guilty after a trial. PMS was used as a mitigating circumstance to obtain a reduced sentence. It succeeded both times, provoking outrage among many British citizens.

Who were these women and what were the circumstances of the murders?

Sandie Smith had over 30 previous convictions, including arson and assault. She had also slashed her wrists on several occasions. Psychiatric reports concluded she was troublesome, an attention-seeker with an "untreatable personality disorder." Her crimes occurred at random and according to one expert "seemed plain mad."

The murder occurred when Sandie Smith got into a fight at a pub and stabbed a barmaid. During the trial, Smith admitted she had not eaten that day. She also had no clear recollection of her behavior. She pleaded innocent but was found guilty of manslaughter.

Dr. Katherina Dalton testified that Smith had PMS based on a diary she had previously kept that indicated her disruptive behavior followed a pattern. Dr. Dalton suggested Sandie Smith could be treated with daily injections of progesterone. Accordingly, Smith was given a probation order of three years, as long as she received the prescribed treatment. Since then, Smith has not behaved violently except in one instance when her dosage was reduced. While some doctors believe progesterone therapy is acting to balance a severe hormone imbalance (one theoretical cause of PMS), other physicians believe progesterone affects the body like a drug—in this case like a powerful tranquilizer that subdues violent impulses. (In the United States, violent male prisoners have been successfully treated with synthetic progesterone.)

There are too many other factors involved (a long previous

criminal record, consistent psychiatric reports, a violent argument at the pub, not eating, causing low blood sugar) to conclude that PMS *alone* caused Smith to stab another person. And even though the hormonal treatment is successful in her case, men, who could not possibly suffer from PMS, have also been treated for compulsive violence with progesterone.

The second case of murder involved a woman with no previous history of uncontrolled violence. Christine English had been involved in a stormy relationship with an alcoholic man. He had frequently beaten her and associated with other women.

On the night of the crime, he had attacked her physically again and threatened to go to another woman. He went out drinking and English went out to look for him. When she found him she pleaded with him to come home, but he demanded she drive him to the other woman's home. The argument continued in the car. He got out of the car, and began to walk away. She attempted to stop him with the car and jammed him against a lamppost. He died two weeks later of multiple internal injuries.

English pleaded guilty to manslaughter.

Several mitigating events were taken into account in her sentencing. First, her period started the morning after the incident, leading to the belief she was premenstrual at the time; she had not eaten for nine hours and she was in a state of extreme anxiety due to the behavior of her lover. Therefore, converging circumstances caused her to do what she did—PMS was only one factor.

Because she was very remorseful about her crime and because the judge felt she had suffered enough through the death of her lover and the subsequent court inquiry, English's sentence was "to eat regularly and abstain from alcohol."

Both cases and their sentences evoked angry criticism in England. To understand the nature of the public outrage, we need to know a little background of current English law. Diminished responsibility, as defined by Great Britain's Homicide Act of 1957, permits convictions of murder to be reduced to charges of manslaughter. It is a kind of middle ground between verdicts of "guilty" and "not guilty by reason of insanity." A guilty verdict means incarceration in a prison; an insanity verdict means confinement in an appropriate mental institution. The "diminished responsibility" verdict allows wide freedom in sentencing.

The law states that "diminished responsibility" may be used in cases when the person who kills is suffering from "such abnormality of mind as substantially impaired his mental responsibility for his acts." However, the law has been liberally interpreted to include various conditions and circumstances. "Diminished responsibility" has been successfully used in England in homicide cases involving deserted spouses, disappointed lovers, depressed people, and sufferers from chronic anxiety. PMS was just another condition added on to a list of others used to commute sentences for killing.

Critics of "diminished responsibility" fear it will go too far. If a person has a migraine, should he be excused for murder? What if a person was just fired from his job? If a person had a bad toothache? If a person simply had an irresistible impulse to kill someone?

There is a profound concern among many British citizens that the punishment for violence against another person is being eroded—in terms of sentencing, tax evasion, fraud, or embezzlement seem to carry stiffer penalties than the taking of human life.

It is a concern in this country, as well, especially now that PMS has been introduced as a defense.

The case that took place in New York City involved Shirley Santos, accused of beating her four-year-old daughter. Her defense attorney, a woman, argued that the charges of child abuse should be dropped because the defendant had PMS.

The prosecuting lawyer, Elizabeth Holtzman, District Attorney of Brooklyn, New York, objected on the basis that there is no evidence women lose control over themselves to the extent that they can't tell right from wrong.

But before the case could be argued in front of the court, Santos gave an interview to a newspaper reporter and told him, "My nerves are not that bad that I am just going to beat up on my kid because my period came down."

As a result, the defense case was hastily dropped. Santos admitted her crime, acknowledging responsibility for her actions.

The chance to argue PMS as a legal defense was lost, but the question remains controversial in the minds of many: Should PMS be used to absolve women of criminal responsibility?

In a recent survey published in *Glamour* magazine, almost three-fourths of readers responding said "no." The reasons against the use of PMS as a defense are numerous.

First and foremost, there is insufficient medical documentation to prove PMS causes violent behavior. Nor is there any evidence that PMS produces "temporary insanity" or the inability to judge right from wrong. Every test done to date on premenstrual women shows that they are lucid, aware, understand events happening around them, and perform well on tests and in other stress situations.

Second, as a result of the "innocent" verdict given to John Hinckley after his assassination attempt on President Ronald Reagan, and other acquittals of violent criminals, there is a growing feeling in this country that mental instability should not be used to excuse criminal behavior. Consequently, in January 1983 the American Psychiatric Association issued a statement urging that acquittals for "insanity" be granted only for *severe abnormal mental disorders* (such as psychosis), and not for personality disorders or antisocial disorders. Even if it could be demonstrated that PMS promotes mental instability or acts as a trigger in certain individuals, that still should not be sufficient grounds for the acquittal of crimes.

Third, PMS as a legal defense is ripe for potential abuse of the condition. The fear is that women could use PMS as an excuse to act monstrously, throw temper tantrums, behave irrationally, destroy property, injure others, and then coolly deny any responsibility for their actions. "PMS made me do it, so don't blame me."

Since there is no medical test to establish whether a woman has PMS or how severely she suffers, a condition of PMS could easily be "invented" as an alibi for murder or any other crime.

Finally, there is the danger that PMS used as a legal defense will boomerang against women. If PMS is ruled to be a medical condition that prevents a sufferer from controlling her behavior, taking responsibility for her actions, or discerning right from wrong, then all women who have PMS will be suspected of being potentially dangerous and "appropriate" precautions would have to be taken: crime could be prevented if women were detained for a week or so every month in a prison ward, an institution, or a home. (Perhaps special premenstrual huts could be built.)

In our society, rights and responsibilities go hand in hand. If a person gives up certain responsibilities, certain rights will also have to be given up. If a person cannot control herself, then, for the safety of society, she will have to be controlled.

As women, as PMS sufferers, we must be on our guard not to fall into this trap.

We must acknowledge that social attitudes toward the entire menstrual process are overwhelmingly negative. In large part, this is due to the fact that in this culture, men are seen as the "norm" and men do not have menstrual cycles: therefore physical processes that only occur in women are thought to be peculiar and abnormal.

Dr. John Money, Professor of Medical Psychology at Johns Hopkins University, warns against the popular trend to pathologize PMS: that is, to consider premenstrual changes as something that require hospitalization or pharmacological treatment. "They've done it to childbirth, they've done it to menopause, and now they're doing it to the menstrual cycle."

One internist quipped that "Menstruation is already considered the curse, now it's premenstrual syndrome, next we'll have *post*-menstrual syndrome." Soon, nothing about being a woman will be considered normal and healthy!

Medical research, which is still conducted primarily by men, is slanted toward the negative. That men, even without the pain and discomfort of PMS and periods, have higher rates of employee absenteeism, industrial accidents, and suicide attempts is not considered. In addition, men are responsible for over 90 percent of all violent acts, criminal behavior, manslaughter, and murder. But no physician or scientist suggests their behavior is due to hormones.

The truth is, there is no sound scientific evidence that links the natural hormonal fluctuations of the menstrual cycle to violence, crime, or even decreased performance.

That is a myth, just as the belief that menstruating women could spoil milk and destroy crops was a myth.

Women are cognitive creatures, Dr. Sommers reminds us, just as men are. All humans have higher centers of reasoning that supersede the lower centers, which control the functioning of our bodies.

The belief that women are dominated by their bodily functions robs them of their unique individuality, the dignity of being considered responsible members of society, and the self-esteem needed to take charge of their own destiny, which is the hallmark of humanity.

But there is good news. With increased knowledge and research about premenstrual syndrome, women can learn to ease or eradicate their symptoms. We can take back control over this part of our health care, our well-being, and our lives.

The rest of this book is dedicated to the many techniques and new discoveries—including diet, exercise, prescription, and nonprescription drugs—that can help you overcome premenstrual syndrome.

8

HOW TO EASE PREMENSTRUAL SYNDROME YOURSELF

My breasts became extremely painful, lumpy, and fibrous the week or so before my period. My gynecologist recommended I stop drinking coffee. Since then, I have cut out almost all caffeine from my diet and I am amazed at the improvement. Now my breasts become only slightly sensitive and the lumps and fibers have completely disappeared.

Helen B., 33
Public-relations executive

Helping Yourself

It is remarkable the number of simple treatments available to reduce particular premenstrual symptoms. In fact, the vast majority of women with PMS can alleviate their own symptoms without the aid of prescription drugs that carry potential side effects, or hormonal therapy, which may upset an already delicate balance.

Helping yourself may seem too simple, too obvious to be true. It is amazing how many women ignore basic premenstrual health care and hope instead to find instant "cures" through pills, suppositories, or injections.

Although some severe PMS sufferers may benefit from prescriptive medicines (see the next chapter to learn more about this option), ultimately the foundation for PMS treatment must be built upon proper premenstrual health management. This is something all women can and should learn.

Dr. Martin Weisberg, a respected gynecologist in private practice, agrees. "Treatment of PMS should involve the whole person. By becoming generally healthier, women can alleviate or even eliminate most premenstrual symptoms."

Not every method suggested in this chapter will help all women. However, many have found relief by trying the treatments offered. These methods of overcoming PMS have been compiled from various doctors, health specialists, and PMS sufferers themselves.

The Foods You Eat

Many major theories concerning the causes of PMS have to do with food. Nutritionists believe that numerous symptoms associated with premenstrual syndrome are the result of an inadequate and improper diet.

For example, too much salt seems to be a major culprit in causing cyclic water retention, producing symptoms ranging from headaches to bloating to irritability.

Periodic hypoglycemia (low blood sugar) can promote premenstrual feelings of nervousness, anxiety, depression, and aggressiveness.

Too much caffeine can cause breast pain and cysts as well as increased anxiety, nervousness, nausea, and altered sleep patterns during the premenstruum.

Women with PMS have special nutritional needs. But the truth is, many women don't get what their bodies require during the premenstrual period. Often PMS sufferers cave in to cravings for sweets and extra salty food. Or there is a tendency to deny themselves and go on self-induced fasts during the premenstrual days.

In general, the American diet contains too much salt, too many artificially sweetened products, and other foods that are overprocessed and robbed of their natural nutritional values. We may not notice the difference during most of the month, but it affects us during the premenstrual phase. (Women, don't despair—our bodies may be more sensitive to nutritional deficiencies, but because our bodies periodically signal us that something is wrong, we can avoid decades of inadequate diet, which often catches up with men during their middle years.)

Most nutritionists agree that women with PMS should pay particular attention to certain nutrients, including calcium, magnesium, vitamins B, C, D, and E, and protein. These are important in synthesizing proper hormonal balance. In addition, iron is essential. Since most women tend to be somewhat anemic during the menstruating years, even a slight iron deficiency can result in premenstrual fatigue and lethargy. For a healthier menstrual cycle, women should eat plenty of iron-rich food throughout the month.

Premenstrual women should practice a secret: *Eat little, but eat often.* Our culture tends to emphasize three hearty meals a day and no snacking. But doctors and nutritionists who have studied PMS recommend that women eat five or six light, well-balanced meals a day, particularly during the premenstrual phase. Some women have found that not only are their PMS symptoms reduced, but they also feel more energetic and actually *lose weight* while using this system.

A light meal might be defined as any food totaling about 250 to 350 calories, based on the average woman's daily intake of 1,800 calories. Although 250 to 350 calories per meal seem minuscule, remember that these mini-meals can and should be eaten every three or four hours, five or six times a day.

Of course the premenstrual diet should be tailored to each individual's caloric requirements, eating preferences, and even work schedules. Some women try breaking up their usual three meals a day into six "mini-meals" or three light meals of 500 calories each with three light snacks of 100 calories each.

The logic behind the practice of eating little but often is that frequent light meals keep blood-sugar levels balanced. Since there seems to be physiological evidence of cyclical hypoglycemia in women, those with PMS would do well to avoid letting blood-sugar levels swing too high or too low. Remember, try not to let more than four or five hours pass without eating something.

By the same token, women with PMS should not fast during their premenstrual phase. Too often, women feel bloated or fat and want to shed a few pounds during this time by fasting. Sometimes PMS can make a woman feel so out of sorts she fasts, hoping to "purge" herself of whatever she believes is causing her distress.

On a psychological level, some women may try to punish their bodies for going through the female cycle by denying themselves through fasting. Others may feel that "not eating" is one way to gain control over a body they perceive as being out of control during the premenstrual phase.

Unfortunately, this is exactly the wrong thing to do during PMS time. Your body has specific nutritional requirements that are especially important as your body prepares to menstruate. Starving yourself can only exacerbate the symptoms and make you feel worse.

On the other hand, many women feel so depleted, physically and emotionally, during the premenstrual week, they overeat. If a woman has a tendency to binge, she'll probably do it most frequently before her period starts. For various physiological reasons, the foods most women crave premenstrually are salty foods, sweet foods, and, to a lesser extent, starches and carbohydrates. Eating, for most of us, fills emotional as well as physical needs. When a woman is feeling depressed, low, unsure of herself—feelings frequently associated with PMS—she may turn to food to console herself, to fulfill unmet psychological needs.

One of the worst things you can do is overindulge in these foods, polishing off a huge piece of chocolate cake, eating chocolate bars, going through a bag of potato chips, stuffing yourself with bread or pasta. This catapults blood-sugar levels to unnatural highs, too much insulin is produced to counteract the excess sugar, and blood-sugar levels plummet again, causing a roller-coaster effect. At a time when your body is coping with premenstrual adjustments, putting your blood-sugar levels on a roller-coaster ride can make it that much harder for you to cope with PMS symptoms.

Furthermore, too much salt, sugar, and carbohydrates usually has the effect of extinguishing a healthy appetite for the proper PMS food—fresh fruits and vegetables, milk, eggs and meat—thereby preventing your body from receiving the nutrients vitally needed during the premenstrual week (protein, calcium, magnesium, vitamins).

But the very worst thing you can do is follow a day of bingeing with a day of fasting. Your body can be thrown completely out of kilter, just when it most needs balance. Some gynecologists have suggested that "bingeing and purging" can radically disrupt hormonal levels, thereby bringing on or intensifying PMS symptoms.

What foods should you eat during the premenstrual phase? Most nutritionists and gynecologists recommend the following:

Fruit juices (fresh or frozen), especially orange juice
Fresh fruit, especially bananas

Fresh and frozen vegetables especially tomatoes (avoid all canned vegetables unless they are salt-free)

Yogurt

Milk (no more than two cups a day)

Eggs (no more than one a day)

Low-salt cheeses, low-salt cottage cheese

Unsalted hot and cold cereals, including puffed wheat, puffed rice, shredded wheat

Breads that are salt-free, especially whole-grain breads

Pasta and rice (no more than one serving a day)

Fresh meat, fish, and fowl (particularly liver)

Unsalted popcorn

Unsalted nuts

Sweet butter or unsalted margarine

Sour cream

Jams, jellies, honey, or maple syrup (no more than one serving a day)

Foods rich in the B vitamins (red meats, milk, eggs, beans, rice)

Foods rich in iron, zinc, and magnesium (liver, poultry, eggs, tomatoes, broccoli, lettuce, mushrooms, and onions)

In general, a sound PMS diet is high in protein, vitamins, and minerals, is moderate in carbohydrates, and very low in salt. The good news is that you can have some sweets, including cake, cookies, Jello, pudding, ice cream, and sherbet. The idea is to have *balanced* blood-sugar levels, not *no* sugar at all. Just be sure to eat only one small to medium sweet treat per day. A small sweet snack can pick up your energy and lift your spirits, especially during premenstrual time when you might be feeling down or tired. It's something to look forward to and won't do any harm, provided the other four or five meals of your day are sensible and nutritious.

The most important thing to remember is to keep away from "instant" foods, prepackaged foods, and canned food. All these contain excess amounts of salt or sugar, which can exacerbate PMS symptoms. Check labels on food. Don't buy anything that includes sugar or corn syrup as one of the first three ingredients and stay away from any product that lists salt.

The best part of the PMS diet is that you don't have to stay on i forever. Just stick to the list during your premenstrual time, how ever many days that may be. Once your period starts, you can retur to your usual eating habits. Some women, though, find they feel s much healthier during their premenstrual time they decide to sta with this diet all month long.

Sound nutrition is not a cure-all for PMS, but it can make a bi difference. The stronger and healthier we are, the better our bodie can cope with premenstrual changes.

Vitamins: Power over PMS

Nutrition is a known factor in PMS management and vitamin play an especially important role in premenstrual health care Some researchers believe that certain vitamin deficiencies ar responsible for many PMS symptoms. Therefore, women wit PMS should make sure they are getting adequate amounts o various vitamins, either through eating vitamin-rich foods or tak ing vitamin supplements.

Vitamin B6

Of all the vitamin deficiencies associated with PMS, the lack o B6 (pyridoxine) is theorized to trigger a hormonal imbalance pro ducing symptoms as diverse as acne, moodiness, nervousnes insomnia, and depression. Some studies have shown that when B is replenished, these symptoms usually lift.

Foods particularly rich in vitamin B6 include meat (especiall liver, pork, and lamb), milk, egg yolks, vitamin-enriched cereal an bread, rice, beans, potatoes, and yeast.

Some doctors recommend women take 25 to 100 mg. of vitamin B6 per day during their premenstrual phase.

Although some physicians prescribe megadoses of vitamin B up to 800 mg. a day, there may be some side effects. Large dail doses of B6 can cause lethargy, insomnia, and physiologica dependency (that is, increasingly higher doses are needed to main tain normal body levels).

Vitamin B₁

Vitamin B₁ (thiamine) is essential to the nervous system, so women who have premenstrual symptoms of nervousness, edginess, and irritability should try to get enough B₁ through their diet. Red meats, carrots, broccoli, spinach, onions, peas, beans, and rice are rich in vitamin B₁. Try taking supplements of 1 mg. to 30 mg. a day during the premenstrual phase. There are no known ill effects associated with large doses of vitamin B₁.

Vitamin B₂

Vitamin B₂ (riboflavin) protects skin and may be instrumental in preventing pre-period pimples, skin rashes, or general itchiness. A severe deficiency of this vitamin can cause diarrhea and even certain mental symptoms. Vitamin B₂ can be found in meat (especially liver), fish, milk, eggs, carrots, broccoli, spinach, and onions. Supplements can be taken from 1 mg. to 30 mg. daily, and there are no known side effects reported from taking large amounts of this vitamin.

Niacin

Niacin is essential for the nervous system and the brain, so to stay at your best during PMS time, you should eat foods rich in niacin: beef, milk, eggs, broccoli, spinach, and onions. The recommended daily allowance is 13 mg., but you may want to try daily amounts up to 100 mg. Large doses (over 50 mg.) may carry some side effects, which include nausea and cramps.

Calcium

Some nutritionists have suggested that calcium deficiency is a major cause of various PMS symptoms and menstrual cramping. Symptoms may be relieved by getting sufficient calcium from milk and other dairy products as well as tomatoes, carrots, broccoli, spinach and other green vegetables. But since the recommended minimum is 800 mg. for women and a cup of milk may contain only 220 mg., it can be almost impossible to meet the daily requirement. Vitamin supplements may therefore be necessary. Daily doses under 2,500 mg. are considered safe, but larger amounts may lead to kidney malfunction.

Iron

Iron is essential to all menstruating women, iron being vital to the healthy development of the uterine lining and menstrual blood. But most women get nowhere near the amount they need, which is a daily minimum of 18 mg. The best nutritional sources for iron are liver, egg yolks, wheat germ, spinach, and broccoli. Supplements can go up to amounts of 200 mg. a day. Higher doses may cause nausea, constipation, or diarrhea.

Vitamin B_{12}

Vitamin B_{12} (cyanocobalamin) is also important to maintaining a healthy nervous system. B_{12} is found in meat and other animal products, such as milk and yogurt. One to three mcg. daily is recommended and there are no side effects associated with larger doses.

Vitamin C

Vitamin C prevents premenstrual muscle pains and skin rashes and may help prevent excessively heavy menstrual periods. Vitamin C can be found especially in citrus fruits, strawberries, tomatoes, carrots, spinach, cauliflower, broccoli, and potatoes. The recommended daily amount is 60 mg. Although megadoses are frequently used and some believe vitamin C is a panacea for everything from the common cold to cancer, large doses may result in temporary physiological dependency, can block the body's absorption of vitamin B_{12} and cause upset stomach, constipation, or diarrhea, as well as the formation of kidney stones.

Vitamin E

Vitamin E is said to help produce ovarian and gonadotropic hormones, essential to a proper hormonal balance. Vitamin E is also important to our muscles and nervous system. Foods rich in vitamin E are nuts (unsalted, of course, during PMS time) and wheat germ as well as eggs and brown rice. The daily minimum requirement is 12 IU and there are no side effects known in doses up to 1,000 IU. One study discovered that women with premenstrual breast cysts found improvement in their condition when they took 600 IU of vitamin E a day.

Vitamin D

Without Vitamin D, our bodies can't absorb calcium, which is thought essential in preventing premenstrual nervousness. Foods that are rich in Vitamin D include fish oils and fortified milk, but much of our Vitamin D is manufactured by our own bodies when exposed to sunlight. Daily allowances have been set at 200 IU. Supplements up to 1,000 IU can be used safely, but larger doses may cause loss of appetite, loss of weight, nausea, constipation, high blood pressure, and calcium deposits in the kidneys.

Most vitamin supplements can be purchased at drugstores or health-food outlets. But even though you don't need a prescription to buy vitamin pills, megadoses may cause more harm than the original symptoms they were meant to cure. You might want to consult with your doctor before taking any vitamin supplements.

The Low-Salt Solution to PMS

Of all the treatments available to women, staying away from salt is one of the most successful solutions to PMS.

Numerous premenstrual symptoms have been directly related to salt and fluid retention. Because of various hormonal changes, women's bodies tend to retain more fluid and salt during the luteal stage of the menstrual cycle. Indeed, many women notice they urinate less before their period. (Usually the start of menstruation is accompanied by an increase of urinary output as the body rids itself of excess water.)

Since salt binds water to cells, women with PMS should reduce their salt intake during the premenstrual period.

This means not adding any salt to your food or to your cooking (if you need to, hide your salt shaker during PMS week!) and not eating obviously salty foods, such as potato chips, pretzels, salted popcorn. But it also means staying away from foods with hidden salt; therefore during the premenstrual phase you should avoid:

Buttermilk

Cheese (except low-sodium cheese)

Processed meats, such as ham, hot dogs, bacon, bologna, "lunch meats"

Anything smoked, dried, pickled, canned, or salted, including tuna, salmon, anchovies, sardines, salt pork, corned beef, herring, caviar, canned shrimp, crab, clams, lobster

Canned vegetables and vegetable juices, sauerkraut

Salted butter and margarine

Peanut butter

Most commercially prepared breads, rolls, cereals (unless made without salt)

Instant cake, pancake, cornbread, muffin mixes

Canned soups, dried soup mixes, boullion cubes

Sodas and soft drinks

Almost all commercially prepared desserts (unless specially prepared without salt)

Condiments such as commercial salad dressings, mayonnaise, gravies, olives, pickles, Worcestershire sauce, soy sauce, catsup, horseradish, relish

Anything containing MSG (monosodium glutamate)

Salt goes by many names, so when you are reading labels, check for not only salt, but also sodium, sodium chloride, bicarbonate of soda, baking powder, sodium benzoate, sodium citrate, and, of course, MSG.

In general, most commercially prepared food products contain a liberal amount of salt. Restaurants usually add too much salt to their food and fast-food establishments are notorious for oversalting everything, even milkshakes. Some gynecologists recommend eating at home during PMS week.

Having PMS doesn't mean you can never again enjoy bacon for breakfast or tuna salad sandwiches for lunch. Just stay away from salty foods during the week to ten days before your period is expected to start. But, generally speaking, reducing your total salt intake throughout the cycle will probably result in an easier week just before menstruation.

Many doctors agree that a low-sodium diet, as simple as it seems, is one of the most effective, safest, and healthiest methods of easing a multitude of PMS symptoms.

Caffeine—Another PMS Culprit

Women with PMS should be cautious about taking caffeine. Caffeine has been implicated in the development of swollen, painful breasts and benign breast cysts. In addition, caffeine increases prostaglandin production (one possible source of many physical PMS symptoms) and can also cause irritability, nervousness, anxiety, sleeplessness, edginess, nausea, and diarrhea, particularly during the PMS period.

Caffeine is found primarily in coffee, but also in tea, chocolate, and chocolate products, and many soft drinks, including colas, orange sodas, lemon/lime sodas, and rootbeers. Caffeine is also an important ingredient in over-the-counter diet pills, "stay-awake" pills, diuretics, analgesics, and, ironically, many drugs for menstrual and premenstrual discomfort.

Even a moderate amount of caffeine can promote premenstrual problems. Some women are extremely sensitive to even small amounts.

Gynecologists have found that one of the best treatments for premenstrual breast pain is to cut out caffeine. Many recommend complete abstention from coffee and tea as being most effective, but some say that even cutting out caffeine for 10 to 14 days before menstruation will be beneficial.

Instead of drinking coffee, tea, or colas, switch to decaffeinated coffee, herbal teas, and sodas that do not contain caffeine (better yet, sparkling mineral water, to avoid sugar).

Giving up caffeine can't cure all PMS symptoms, but it will most likely decrease or eliminate pre-period breast pain and cysts. It may also eradicate feelings of anxiety and edginess. Avoiding caffeine is safe, simple, and it may very well reduce some premenstrual discomfort.

About Diuretics

Water retention is very common during the premenstrual phase, and although reducing salt intake can relieve much of the bloating and the discomfort that comes with it, some women find that a low-salt diet is just not enough. Therefore, doctors who treat PMS often suggest that the low-salt diet be accompanied by nonprescription diuretics.

Some of the leading brands include Aqua-Ban, Cardui, Femcaps, Midol, Pamprin, Permathene H2OFF, Pre-Mens Forte, Sunril, and Trendar. The diuretic drugs they contain are ammonium chloride, pamabrom, or caffeine in doses lower than 100 mg. The American Pharmaceutical Association describes caffeine under 100 mg. as a weak diuretic and over 100 mg. as a stimulant. (If breast swelling and cysts, nervousness, and irritability are part of your PMS symptoms, avoid diuretics that contain caffeine. Check the product label.) In addition, Femcaps and Midol contain muscle relaxers, which may alleviate premenstrual abdominal pain.

Some words of caution: Diuretics should not be used by individuals with high blood pressure, heart or kidney disease. Also, do not take aspirin while using diuretics. Ammonium chloride (the leading ingredient in many over-the-counter diuretics) slows the elimination of aspirin from the body. Use acetaminophen instead.

Herbal diuretics are popular especially with those women who prefer to try a more "natural" approach to premenstrual problems. Many herbal teas are on the market as well as over-the-counter diuretics made from herbal products. Some of the better known herbal diuretics are Lydia Pinkham's Vegetable Compound, Naturade K.B.11, Odrinil and Nature's Bounty Water Pill Tablets. They include a diversity of ingredients, such as buchu leaves, corn silk, dandelion, horsetail, juniper berries, and watermelon seeds.

The effectiveness of these products has never been proved, but taken in recommended amounts, they are safe. Still, don't overdo these herbal diuretics even though they are "natural." Anything strong enough to draw water out of body cells should be treated with respect and not abused.

The same can be said for herbal teas. The most popular for use as a diuretic are buchu leaves, dandelion, and elder bark. Plants and vegetables such as parsley, watercress, celery, and cucumber are also mild diuretics that may help flush body tissues' extra fluid.

In spite of the lack of scientific evidence supporting the actual effectiveness of diuretics, herbal or otherwise, in the treatment of premenstrual syndrome, millions of women have found relief through their use.

Remember, if you do decide to try a diuretic, take it only during your premenstrual phase and stop as soon as your period starts.

As in anything, use common sense while taking diuretics. Even the best products will not do much good if you have just eaten a large bag of potato chips.

In addition, stop using the diuretic if you notice any side effects, such as rapid pulse, heart palpitations, dizziness, unusual weakness or tiredness, headache, abdominal pain, nausea, diarrhea, or vomiting. These symptoms may mean the particular diuretic you are using is not suitable for you or that diuretics in general cannot be tolerated by your body's system. You may want to contact your doctor.

Analgesics and PMS

Premenstrual symptoms can be soothed by relatively mild nonprescription drugs. What are they? The best and most effective are simple analgesics: aspirin and acetaminophen. Both relieve premenstrual pain.

Aspirin works as an anti-prostaglandin agent and an anticoagulant, which may prevent the pain associated with clots passing through the cervical opening during menstruation. Some doctors recommend taking aspirin for several days before menstruation to inhibit the production of prostaglandin.

Although aspirin has a multitude of positive effects for the PMS sufferer, it is not without some side effects, of which you should be aware.

Aspirin should never be used if you are also taking anticoagulants, since both reduce blood clotting and may cause hemorrhaging. In addition, individuals with ulcers should not use aspirin, since it may produce stomach bleeding. Aspirin can also cause allergic reactions, skin rashes, respiratory symptoms, and gastric upset leading to ulcers.

If you notice ringing in your ears while taking aspirin, discontinue it immediately as this side effect may indicate an overdose.

You should consult with your doctor before using aspirin if you are also taking antacids, diabetic medication, antibiotics, cortisone, blood-pressure medication, and sulfa drugs. In addition, diuretics containing ammonium chloride and large doses of vitamin C should not be taken if you are using aspirin since these substances can multiply the effects of aspirin by slowing its elimination from the body.

Acetaminophen, found in such products as Datril, Femcaps, Pamprin, and Tylenol, is often used as a substitute for aspirin, especially by those who cannot tolerate aspirin. Acetaminophen works as an anticoagulant but does not cause stomach bleeding. It is not considered an effective anti-prostaglandin agent, and it will not reduce inflammation.

The major side effects to be aware of when taking acetaminophen are nausea, vomiting, chills, and drowsiness. Overdoses can lead to liver or kidney damage.

Most of the side effects associated with aspirin and acetaminophen happen only rarely. The vast majority of women can and do use these simple, common, but effective drugs to relieve headaches, abdominal pain, joint pain, and other minor aches and pains associated with premenstrual syndrome.

The Effect of Exercise on PMS

One of the more effective ways to manage PMS is through exercise. Dancers and athletes rarely have premenstrual problems. However, most women in our culture are woefully out of condition. Premenstrual tension and lethargy can make a woman feel like giving up completely, but that's the worst way to handle PMS.

Exercise has multiple benefits for women with PMS. It's a way to relax after a stressful day. It keeps your mind off and actually reduces cravings for sugary, high carbohydrate foods. It builds up muscles and general bodily strength to help cope with premenstrual syndrome. It promotes blood circulation, and hence an increased feeling of well-being. Most important, it helps a woman feel she is in control of her body.

Doctors give medical reasons for starting a regular exercise program. The flow of hormonal secretions seems to be regulated by exercise. Mild premenstrual depression and fatigue can also be overcome through exercise. In addition, since fatty tissues store excessive amounts of estrogen, becoming slimmer and more muscular by exercising regularly can help keep hormones balanced.

There is no reason to think women cannot exercise or participate in sports during the premenstruum or during menstruation. The problem is women *think* they can't do as well or they feel too lethargic to even try. Even some female athletic champions believe that the menstrual cycle affects their performance. But in reality, American Olympic champions have won medals at all phases of the cycle. There is simply no statistical or medical evidence to show a woman can't win a gold medal or a tennis game, or a bicycle race, or a dance competition during PMS time.

Still, many women approach the mere thought of exercising with apprehension, especially around the time of menstruation. Relax, you needn't start a zealous exercise program all at once. After all, the body's condition after years of inactivity can only be changed slowly and steadily.

Fortunately, there are many ways to exercise and you have the opportunity to choose that which is most effective and most appealing to you.

Of all the exercises, breathing exercises, yoga, and swimming are most recommended to alleviate and even prevent premenstrual symptoms. Join a gym or a health spa. But if you'd like to try something else, browse through your library or favorite bookstore for books on exercise. Dozens are in print and available. You might just find an exercise program that works for you.

Exercise can bring both physical and mental benefits. Jogging, swimming, dancing, gardening, aerobics, hiking, yoga, bicycling, and even walking can help eliminate premenstrual aches and "slumps" by keeping you in good general health while ridding your body and spirit of stress and tension.

PMS and Sex

Having an orgasm is a powerful and pleasureful way to relieve premenstrual tension and irritability. In addition, the sexual play that precedes an orgasm can be especially exciting and fulfilling during the premenstrual phase.

Masters and Johnson demonstrated that women are most easily aroused at that time and reach the sexual plateau more quickly. Other independent researchers have confirmed their work. Indeed, many women agree that sex is best before their period.

Beyond the physical release that is achieved through an orgasm, sexual relations can also soothe and satisfy the spirit.

Touching, embracing, feeling the warmth of the person you love are greatly comforting. Knowing your partner loves you and cares about you can ease some of the self-doubt and depression that sometimes accompany PMS. When you feel achy and out of sorts, it is reassuring to receive affection and tenderness.

It is important that women give themselves permission to enjoy the body's natural increase in sexual desire.

Unfortunately, even in today's "liberated" climate, a significant number of women still do not have an orgasm during sexual intimacy for reasons ranging from faulty technique to repression of sexual feelings to fear of being out of control at the moment of climax.

Some psychologists and gynecologists believe that this can contribute to premenstrual tension and other PMS symptoms, including irritability, displaced aggression, muscular tension, and abdominal pain. Some theorize that hormonal therapy works by decreasing libido—if "unacceptable" sexual urges are taken away, the resulting tension and other symptoms disappear.

Although deep-seated sexual problems should be treated in a psychological or sexual therapy setting, some women can begin to overcome premenstrual sexual tension through masturbation. Several excellent books have been written on this subject. Learning to accept your sexuality and control your own sexual pleasure is one way to begin to accept your womanliness and alleviate some premenstrual symptoms.

You don't always need a doctor's prescription to cope with PMS. There are many ways to overcome those unpleasant pre-period symptoms and the more methods you can incorporate into your life style, the more successful you will probably be in controlling PMS. To summarize:

- *Eat little, but often.* Hormone levels change throughout the cycle, but after ovulation the female body becomes more susceptible to hypoglycemia. To keep your blood-sugar levels even, eat five or six small meals a day. Try not to go more than four hours without food.
- *Get sufficient vitamins.* Some experts believe hormonal imbalance is brought on by vitamin deficiencies, especially a deficiency of vitamin B_6. Get the vitamins you need through the food you eat or take vitamin supplements.
- *Stay away from salt.* Since salt binds water to body cells, and water retention is one major cause of many PMS symptoms, reducing your salt intake should alleviate premenstrual bloating and associated symptoms. Don't add salt to your food at the table or while cooking and avoid commercially prepared food high in sodium.
- *Cut down on caffeine.* Caffeine has been implicated in connection with cystic, fibrous, and swollen breasts as well

as premenstrual edginess and irritability. Avoid not only coffee, but tea, chocolate, and colas.

- *Be aware of alcohol's effects.* Women's bodies absorb alcohol more rapidly after ovulation, so be careful with the amounts you drink. Half as much can make you twice as high.

- *Try nonprescription medication.* Over-the-counter diuretics may help flush excess water when a low-salt diet doesn't quite do the trick. (But if breast pain, edginess, and irritability are major symptoms, be careful of over-the-counter drugs containing caffeine.) Take diuretics only during your premenstrual time. Discontinue them after your period starts. Analgesics such as aspirin and acetaminophen can alleviate specific physical premenstrual aches and pains. Use these drugs in moderation and as directed.

- *Exercise.* PMS can't be cured lying down. Exercise will help keep your body in good condition in order to combat PMS symptoms. Some physicians believe that a regular exercise regime can even banish many premenstrual and menstrual problems. Don't give in to feelings of lethargy. Women with PMS should exercise all month long.

- *Enjoy an orgasm.* Premenstrual tension and pelvic congestion can be relieved by having an orgasm. Making love with a caring partner can also soothe and lift your spirit.

- *Get enough rest.* Women may need extra sleep premenstrually, so schedule an hour's nap or go to bed a little earlier during that time. You'll have much more energy and physical reserves to cope with PMS symptoms.

9

MEDICAL ADVANCES AND TREATMENTS OF PREMENSTRUAL SYNDROME

I saw an ad in the newspaper about a new clinic which treats PMS. After suffering for twenty years with this, I was eager to learn something about it. I took my fourteen-year-old daughter with me to their introductory session for prospective patients. We were shown a film about women who have premenstrual syndrome. Afterward, my daughter said, "That's it! That's it! That's what you're like, Mommy. You've got to sign up for this!"

Irene P., 44
Bank officer

Prescription Treatments for PMS

Many new prescription treatments are being offered today to women who suffer from PMS. Furthermore, clinics and centers for premenstrual syndrome are springing up around the country. They offer hope, counseling, and cures. For some, the treatments do seem to help and provide relief. For others, the results are disappointing and costly.

Unfortunately, none of these treatments have been scientifically proven as cures for PMS. In fact, when scrutinized under carefully controlled, double-blind scientific studies, most treatments have been found to be no more effective in treating premenstrual syndrome than sugar pills (placebos). Furthermore, some medicines may even prove to be harmful, especially if used over an extended period of time. No evidence is yet available as to the long-term effects of these treatments for premenstrual syndrome.

At the same time, it cannot be denied that some women have found relief from premenstrual syndrome by using these medications. Their symptoms have become manageable, perhaps permitting normal life activities for the first time in years. These women feel that the benefits of the treatments outweigh any possible detriments.

This chapter will examine the variety of treatments available, taking a look at the pros and cons. Because some doctors are convinced that only their treatment is the right one or are unaware of other methods, it is extremely important for women to understand why a particular drug is being prescribed and what possible benefits they can expect.

By understanding the options, the drugs available, and their side effects, a woman seeking treatment from a clinic or a doctor will be better informed and more capable of making a decision concerning her health care.

Prescriptive Diuretics

Diuretics are the most prescribed form of treatment of premenstrual syndrome. Some would say they are the most *over*prescribed. Those critical of prescription diuretics maintain that the same results could be achieved by dietary changes—that is, reducing salt intake—and occasionally by using milder over-the-counter diuretics.

However, in some cases these self-help measures may not be enough. When a low-salt diet and nonprescription diuretics do not seem to alleviate the bloating and its related symptoms, a woman may want to try something stronger.

Because prescriptive diuretics are powerful drugs that carry several potentially dangerous side effects, they should be used only for about one week before the expected start of menstruation. Once bleeding begins, the shift in hormones causes fluids to drain away naturally. Many women notice that on the first day or so of menstruation they begin to urinate frequently and copiously.

PMS cannot be cured by using diuretics all month long—they may, in fact, interfere with the body's natural hormonal and fluid balances. Since diuretics are prescribed for various conditions and diseases, be sure to tell your doctor that your bloating is related to your menstrual cycle, so that he or she can tailor the prescription accordingly.

The diuretics most recommended and prescribed are Lasix (furosemide) and the group of related drugs called the thiazides. Their brand names include Diuril, Esidrix, and Hydrodiural. The possile side effects include lightheadedness, dizziness, loss of appetite, nausea, diarrhea, vomiting, and allergic reactions, particularly ashes and hives.

The side effect that is common to almost all diuretics is the possible loss of potassium. When large amounts of bodily fluids are artificially washed out through the use of drugs, the body's supply of potassium can be radically depleted. The consequences of potassium depletion are feelings of weakness and lethargy, muscle aches, cramps and spasms, heart palpitations, and, in extreme cases, sudden death. (Diuretics should not be used if there is the possibility of pregnancy, as the drugs can damage the developing fetus.)

To prevent potassium depletion, doctors recommend eating foods rich in potassium. Fortunately, most foods on the list are low in salt and are perfect for the PMS diet. (The fruits and vegetables should be fresh or frozen, not canned.)

Bananas	Potatoes
Citrus fruits	Spinach
Dried apricots	Milk
Peaches	Beef
Prunes	Chicken
Raisins	Fish
Carrots	Liver
Lentils	Pork
Lima beans	Unsalted almonds
Tomatoes	Unsalted peanut butter
Broccoli	Unsalted all-bran
Eggplant	cereals and breads
Lettuce	

Some gynecologists prefer to prescribe Aldactone (spironolactone) or Dyrenium (triamterene) for menstrual-related water retention as neither of these diuretics causes potassium depletion. In fact, if using these drugs, doctors recommend that potassium supplements *not* be taken and patients should not eat any more potassium-rich foods than they usually would. Although these diuretics have the benefit of keeping potassium levels stable, they still carry the possibility of side effects common to the other diuret ics. In addition, Aldactone may cause menstrual irregularities in some women. If one diuretic doesn't agree with you or you expe rience unpleasant side effects, ask your doctor for a different drug Another prescription may work better for you.

Very infrequently, serious adverse effects result from taking any of the diuretic drugs. Discontinue the diuretic immediately and notify your doctor if you notice any of the following: severe skin reactions indicating allergy, jaundice indicating liver damage severe abdominal pain indicating pancreas inflammation, or a group of symptoms including fatigue, fever, sore throat, and unus ual bleeding or bruising indicating bone-marrow depression.

Common sense should prevail when taking diuretics. Don't use this medicine as an excuse to overeat or binge on salty foods thinking that the diuretics will wash it all away. And never take more than the recommended amount, thinking more pills will mean more relief. Even a moderate diuretic overdose can cause extreme thirst, lethargy, weakness, muscle pain, and cramps defeating the entire purpose of PMS treatment. Large overdoses can lead to stupor and coma.

Prescription diuretics are powerful and may be unnecessarily powerful in most PMS cases. Some studies have questioned the effectiveness of strong diuretics for PMS treatment. There seems to be a placebo effect (that is, patients taking placebos, or sugar pills report approximately the same amount of relief as patients taking the medication). Nonetheless, there are women who have found diuretics to be their only salvation, relieving premenstrual symp toms from bloating to breast swelling to irritability to headaches to mood changes. Used cautiously, under a doctor's supervision, with potassium levels kept stable, diuretics can be worth the try.

Valium and Other Tranquilizers

Tranquilizing drugs are widely prescribed by doctors in the treatment of premenstrual syndrome; however, they may worsen many of the symptoms without curing others.

Some doctors prescribe tranquilizers because they believe the underlying cause of premenstrual distress is emotional tension or anxiety. Tranquilizers may vanquish those feelings and thereby reduce PMS symptoms. Other studies have found that when PMS is largely psychological in origin or due to personality problems, neurosis, or psychosis, a variety of tranquilizing agents may help when coupled with psychotherapy. However, psychotherapy or other psychological therapies used alone are considered to be ineffective in treating PMS. On the other hand, doctors may be unaware of or unfamiliar with other causes or treatments of PMS and so prescribe tranquilizers.

Because tranquilizers act as depressants, they can worsen such PMS symptoms as lethargy and depression. If those are your primary premenstrual problems, tranquilizers are not the answer for you. If premenstrual depression is overwhelming, your doctor may want to consider prescribing an antidepressant drug to be used only during the premenstrual days.

The possible side effects of tranquilizers include drowsiness and a feeling of unsteadiness. Occasionally, skin rashes, dizziness, blurred vision, slurred speech, and menstrual irregularities may occur. Paradoxically, Valium can produce agitation, hostility, and rage, the very PMS symptoms this tranquilizer may have been prescribed to cure.

There is a high factor of addiction present in using tranquilizers; but dependency can be avoided if they are used sparingly and only during the premenstrual phase when symptoms appear. As a treatment for PMS, tranquilizers should not be taken every day of the cycle. In addition, as they may cause drowsiness, patients should exercise caution at work or when driving. Do not drink alcohol while using tranquilizers. The combined effect of the drug, plus alcohol, plus the body's reduced tolerance for alcohol during PMS time, can prove harmful and possibly fatal.

However, used with caution under a doctor's care, the minor tranquilizers may be helpful if the predominant premenstrual symptoms seem to include anxiety, irritability, hostility, tension, or restlessness.

Ponstel and Other Anti-Prostaglandin Drugs

Some physicians believe prostaglandins (the proven culprit in painful menstrual cramping) may also cause premenstrual syndrome. Although initial research indicates that anti-prostaglandin drugs alleviate many physical symptoms such as cramping, breast tenderness, and other premenstrual aches, they have not been shown to be effective in curing the psychological symptoms, such as tension and depression.

However, since for many women the physical symptoms are the worst, they may want to discuss anti-prostaglandin treatment with their physician.

Anti-prostaglandin drugs work to inhibit the body's production of prostaglandins (the hormone-like substances that cause contractions and sometimes pain in the smooth muscles, such as the uterus). Prostaglandin-inhibiting drugs are far more effective than aspirin, but they also have more side effects.

Here is what women should know about these drugs:

ANAPROX (naproxen)—the first prostaglandin successfully used to treat menstrual cramps. May cause headache, dizziness, drowsiness, vomiting, indigestion, bloating, skin problems, depression, and gastric bleeding. Don't take aspirin with Anaprox, as they counter each other's effect. Should not be used if pregnant or nursing.

INDOCIN (indomethacin)—used primarily to treat arthritis, but has been used experimentally for menstrual distress. May cause urinary problems, weight gain, depression, skin rashes, itching, headache, drowsiness, dizziness, loss of appetite, vomiting, hair loss, gastric bleeding and kidney failure. Should not be taken with diuretics. Do not take during pregnancy or while nursing.

MOTRIN (ibuprofen)—relieves moderate but not extreme menstrual pain. May promote urinary difficulties, headache, nausea, lethargy, fluid retention, skin problems, depression, hives, stomach irritation, and gastric bleeding.

NALFON (fenoprofen)—works as a painkiller and as an

anti-inflammatory agent. May cause stomach irritation, allergic reactions, urinary problems, skin problems, depression, headaches, confusion, ringing in ears, nausea, constipation, and gastric bleeding.

PONSTEL (mefenamic acid)—a powerful painkiller with the fewest adverse reactions, primarily rash, urinary difficulties and kidney disease. Many gynecologists consider this their drug of choice in treating premenstrual and menstrual distress.

All of the above drugs may cause an upset stomach. And, as in any drug, there is always the chance of an allergic reaction in an individual sensitive to that particular medication. In addition, some patients have noticed decreased concentration while using anti-prostaglandins. It is generally suggested that alcohol be used with moderation if at all while taking these drugs as the combination may increase the risk of stomach bleeding or ulceration.

Since each prostaglandin-inhibiting drug is slightly different, your doctor may suggest you try several to find the one that works best for you.

To prevent painful menstrual cramping, start taking the prostaglandin-inhibiting medication several days before your period starts. Premenstrual symptoms can be alleviated if the drugs are used anywhere from three to ten days before menstruation. Patients using anti-prostaglandin drugs in the treatment of PMS have found significant relief from breast pain, joint pain, abdominal bloating and cramping, swollen wrists and ankles, headaches, nausea, and general discomfort.

Painkillers

Doctors often prescribe painkillers such as codeine, Percodan, Talwin, Darvon, and the Darvon compounds for premenstrual problems or menstrual pain. Frequently, patients ask for these painkillers and won't be satisfied until they have the prescription. Surprisingly, medical tests have shown that none of these drugs is any more effective than simple, common aspirin.

Nonetheless, women ask for the prescription painkillers because they think these drugs are stronger and more powerful than something that can be purchased at any drugstore and supermarket. Indeed, the placebo effect may be at work here. But some physicians have the philosophy, "It doesn't matter how it works or whether it works, as long as the patient believes it works and gets relief."

So, if you've thought about trying prescriptive painkillers or your doctor has suggested them as a treatment for PMS, you should be aware of the possible side effects.

All the prescription painkillers can be habit forming. They are narcotics and therefore can cause addiction and strong withdrawal symptoms when the drug is stopped. Therefore, when used to relieve PMS pain, they should be taken only during the premenstrual phase and discontinued immediately after the start of menstruation.

Other side effects include allergic reactions, upset stomach, lightheadedness, drowsiness, nausea, constipation, vomiting, headache, agitation, insomnia, and behavioral disturbances. Never use codeine with a diuretic; the combination can cause a serious drop in blood pressure. Avoid alcohol as well—used with codeine, the combination may cause a severe depressant effect on brain, respiratory, and circulation functions.

Prescription painkillers may relieve premenstrual physical pain associated with PMS, but they will not have a direct effect on emotional symptoms.

Parlodel

Parlodel (bromocriptine) is a new drug that inhibits the release of prolactin, a hormone suspected by some researchers to be the cause of PMS. European doctors have had some success in treating PMS patients with bromocriptine, but other studies show only mixed results.

Parlodel is an extremely powerful drug with numerous serious side effects, including nausea, visual disturbances, and a drop in blood pressure.

This drug seems to be most effective in controlling premenstrual breast swelling and soreness. If breast pain is your major PMS symptom, you may want to discuss this medication with your doctor.

Oral Contraceptives

The use of oral contraceptives, or birth-control pills, as a treatment for PMS is a medical paradox. Some women find enormous relief, others find their symptoms horribly worsened. There hardly seems to be a middle ground. Either oral contraceptives do just the trick—reducing bloating, eliminating breast cysts and swelling, steadying mood swings, eradicating physical pain—or they create a hormonal nightmare—deep depression, severe headaches, extreme nausea, constant menstrual bleeding.

Contraceptive pills contain synthetic hormones, which replace the body's production of estrogen and progesterone. Most doctors believe that when the Pill works, it does so by suppressing ovulation and keeping hormone levels steady. Ovulation is associated with painful periods and some premenstrual symptoms. Some researchers believe that women who do not ovulate rarely experience premenstrual syndrome. Eliminating hormonal fluctuations also prevents the pre-period water retention that seems to cause so many PMS symptoms. For some women, simply knowing their next period won't be painful because they are taking the Pill causes a reduction in pre-period anxiety, depression, edginess, or tension due to the anticipation of pain. Hence, women are better able to cope with other PMS symptoms.

On the other hand, when oral contraceptives don't work, they suddenly and dramatically multiply PMS symptoms. The most common side effects include the onset of depression, irritability, headaches, and nausea. Sometimes bloating, breast swelling, and menstrual abnormalities also appear. Women with PMS who cannot tolerate the Pill usually report that the side effects began within a short period of time after they started oral contraceptives. In a few cases, the symptoms began within one to three days.

For various reasons, some women continue taking the Pill in spite of the side effects. Some stay on oral contraceptives for months or even years. When they finally discontinue the pills, they find they have a full-blown case of PMS.

Therefore, if oral contraceptives are suggested as treatment for premenstrual symptoms and you notice any of the above side effects, stop taking the Pill immediately. These disturbing symptoms are the body's way of shouting "Something is wrong!" Don't let a doctor convince you that you'll "adjust" or "adapt" to the pills. You may not, and your natural hormonal cycle can be permanently upset.

Unfortunately, it is impossible to predict which woman will benefit from birth control pills and which will suffer ill effects. However, since many women gain definite relief when taking oral contraceptives, it may make sense to try this medication as a treatment for PMS. Since different types of birth-control pills have different chemical compositions, your gynecologist may suggest switching brands to find the one that works best for you.

Oral contraceptives are contraindicated for women with a history of blood clots, varicose veins, diabetes, liver trouble, heart disease, and glandular disease. Furthermore, many gynecologists feel the Pill is not advisable for women over 35, especially those who smoke cigarettes.

Be sure to ask your doctor about possible side effects and read the instruction sheet that comes with each packet of pills. It defines all known problems associated with the birth-control pill. If you are one of those women who cannot tolerate the Pill, you'll probably find out before the first cycle of pills is completed. But if you can take the Pill without incurring those troublesome side effects, it may be an effective way to overcome PMS.

Progestogens

Some doctors believe that PMS is caused by a deficiency of progesterone, or a relative deficiency of this hormone in relation to an excess of estrogen. They theorize that supplements of progesterone will bring the two hormones back into balance.

Based on this belief, some doctors prescribe progestogen pills (a synthetic progesterone drug). These pills do not contain estrogen, as do oral contraceptives, and are usually taken only during the premenstrual phase.

Some studies in England have shown that women treated with progestogens received significant relief from their premenstrual symptoms, particularly water retention, migraine, anxiety, irritability, and hostility.

However, the use of synthetic progesterone has been criticized by many in the medical community. Other researchers doubt the validity of the progesterone deficiency theory, citing several studies that show progestogens actually work like tranquilizers. They seem to reduce anxiety and decrease aggressive impulses and violent behavior. (Experiments with violent male criminals who volunteered to take progestogens demonstrated a remarkable decrease in hostility.)

Still other medical researchers point out that there has never been a double-blind controlled trial demonstrating that progestogen treatment is any more effective than placebos in treating PMS.

As with any hormone treatment, there are often side effects. They range from breast tenderness to menstrual irregularities to more serious problems of blood clots and cardiovascular complications, as well as suspected links to cancer. Ironically, progestogen treatment sometimes exacerbates the very premenstrual symptoms it is supposed to cure.

Synthetic progesterone may help some women, but because of the multiple health risks, it should be prescribed with great caution and only when other less drastic methods have failed.

Because of the numerous side effects associated with large doses of progestogens, a few gynecologists have experimented by treating their PMS patients with very small doses of synthetic progesterone, sometimes by prescribing the "mini-pill."

Women trying mini-pills should be aware of their unproven and experimental status. Even minute amounts of progestogens can produce some unwanted side effects, notably irregular menstrual bleeding. Still, doctors who have prescribed this treatment report considerable success, without the risks inherent in large doses of hormones.

Progesterone Therapy

The natural hormone progesterone has been acclaimed as the most effective treatment for premenstrual syndrome and is considered to be superior to synthetic progesterone.

Of all the treatments, progesterone therapy has gained the most publicity. But what many women do not know is that a considerable number of doctors and medical researchers have questioned the efficacy and the safety of this treatment. Because some women with PMS may be influenced to try progesterone, or are already using it without fully understanding the doubts and dangers involved, it is very important to deal with the issue of progesterone therapy here.

Natural progesterone is a treatment endorsed by Dr. Katherina Dalton, the English clinician, and several physicians in this country whose names have been prominently associated with PMS treatments.

Dr. Dalton is responsible for popularizing the progesterone deficiency theory, notably in her book *Once a Month,* which is crammed with case histories of women with symptoms from the benign to the most bizarre who have been cured by taking progesterone supplements. The book is based on Dr. Dalton's experience in treating thousands of women with PMS.

In order for the treatment to be effective, according to Dr. Dalton and her followers, progesterone must be given in doses far higher than the amount physiologically produced by the average woman during the course of a normal menstrual cycle. Hormonal megadoses do not seem to concern the doctors who advocate this treatment because (1) they claim it works and (2) they justify the high levels by explaining that during pregnancy progesterone soars to even higher levels than are administered in this PMS therapy.

Furthermore, (3) the progesterone is "natural" and is, presumably, safe to use.

Progesterone is manufactured from yams and soybean plants. It cannot be taken in pill form because the natural hormone is too quickly broken down by the digestive system and excreted from the body before it can take full effect.

So far, the only way to take natural progesterone is by injection or by suppositories, which are inserted into the vagina or the rectum. Some new forms include a liquid to be inserted into the rectum and a powder that can be placed under the tongue or in the vagina.

The treatment is admittedly unpleasant. Women say the injections are painful, the suppositories are leaky and sometimes cause vaginal or rectal burning and irritation, the powder is bitter and gritty, and the fluid must be inserted with a turkey basting syringe (!). As one journalist remarked, "You'd have to be desperate to take the stuff."

But some women with PMS are desperate and will eagerly try anything that promises premenstrual relief.

Doctors who prescribe progesterone suppositories usually recommend that women begin with a 200 mg. suppository each day during the premenstrual phase. (Compare this dosage with the .3 mg. to 2 mg. used in most birth-control pills.) But if that massive dosage doesn't work, the amount is increased to 400 mg. a day and up. There are women taking 1,600 mg. of progesterone daily.

In general, patients are encouraged to take whatever amount they feel is needed for as long as they think necessary. Physicians who prescribe this treatment admit it is still experimental and therefore no one knows for sure how much an individual woman might require to overcome her PMS symptoms.

Many physicians and researchers, however, have their doubts. They suspect progesterone treatment may turn out to be not only ineffective, but harmful as well. Before trying progesterone therapy, women should be aware of the controversy surrounding this treatment and some of the possible dangers.

• *The very thesis that a progesterone deficiency causes PMS has been questioned by many.* There is no direct proof that a certain percentage of women have a hormonal deficiency, as described by Dr. Dalton. The truth is, studies carried out to date have been unable to demonstrate any discernible difference between hormone levels of women with severe PMS and those with little or no premenstrual problems. Progesterone deficiency has not been proven to cause PMS and there are no medical tests available to show the existence of PMS. The routine blood tests recommended by doctors treating PMS can only indicate the most severe hormonal imbalances. One gynecologist commented, "If a hormonal abnormality showed up in one of those tests, that women would have such troubles, PMS would be the least of her worries."

● *Doctors, even those who prescribe progesterone, do not fully understand how it works.* Some believe it is acting to make up a deficiency, much like insulin injections in cases of diabetes. But others suspect it acts as a drug, such as Valium. There is some evidence to suggest that massive doses of progesterone have a tranquilizing effect on the nervous system.

● *Comparing megadoses of progesterone with the high levels of progesterone produced during pregnancy is misleading.* Obstetricians and gynecologists point out that during pregnancy, many other hormones rise proportionately and may counteract or balance progesterone's effects. There are many things that go on during pregnancy that medical scientists are only dimly aware of; artificially increasing only one of those elements cannot be compared with the increases that happen naturally during pregnancy.

● *That progesterone is natural and therefore safe is inaccurate.* First, there is nothing natural about shooting one of the body's hormones up to hundreds of times its normal level. Second, what may be safe at low physiological levels may be dangerous at higher pharmaceutical levels.

● *Studies done to date on progesterone therapy have yet to prove it is any more effective than a placebo.* Dr. Dalton herself has never done a controlled double-blind study of her treatment, and although several have tried, no one has ever been able to duplicate her claims of success. In general, her work has been criticized by the scientific community for its lack of statistical evaluation and its serious methodological errors. This has caused many to doubt her work and the efficacy of progesterone treatment.

● *Numerous alarming side effects have been associated with progesterone use.* Some of the more serious adverse reactions include:

— Mood swings
— Restlessness or sleeplessness
— Dizziness or fainting
— Muscle spasms
— Chest pains
— Decreased sex drive
— Vaginal infections
— Uterine cramping
— Altered menstrual cycles
— Change in menstrual flow
— Cessation of menstruation
— Continuous menstrual bleeding

There are women who have not had a period since they started taking progesterone and women who bleed constantly, every day of the month. Another strange side effect is that the PMS symptoms get pushed into the formerly symptom-free period. The chances for and the severity of these side effects seem to multiply as the treatment is continued or the doses are increased.

● *There are no set, monitored dosages of progesterone.* Women who take progesterone use 200 mg. a day, 200 mg. three times a day, 400 mg. four times a day, or whatever. Most doctors advise women to regulate themselves. "You have to find the dose that's right for you." No other prescription medicine is treated with such casualness. Many members of the medical community are concerned that this approach has lead some women to become "progesterone junkies."

● *Some doctors suspect the very serious possibility of progesterone addiction.* Many women find they must have increasingly larger doses of this medication for increasingly longer periods of time. More than a few women are taking 1,600 mg. of progesterone every day of the month.

It is common for women to report experiencing a "rush" of well-being, of euphoria, after taking progesterone. Marnie G., 35, a salesclerk, describes her experience:

> *About ten minutes after I put in the suppository, I am flooded with a feeling of calmness. I feel tranquil and at peace. All my pain disappears.*

But several hours later the user often experiences a "crash," as many women call it. They talk of a horrible letdown, a sudden dive into despair, a tidal wave of pain.

So, to avoid this feeling, some women begin taking their dosages more frequently. Other women dread the "crashes" so much, they use progesterone every day, all month long. Almost all these women experience numerous side effects, but too often their doctors reassure them, saying, "You just haven't found the right dosage yet." Some women do become "scared to death," to use one woman's expression, and stop using progesterone.

● *The Federal Drug Administration has not approved progesterone in doses over 200 mg. a day or for use as treatment for PMS.* The FDA has not sanctioned the use of progesterone for treatment of PMS because of studies indicating possible links to cancer. Progesterone has been shown to produce malignant tumors in animals. Synthetic progesterone has already been associated with blood clots, cardiovascular problems, as well as cancer of the reproductive organs; natural progesterone in high enough doses may produce the same effects. After experiences with thalidomide, DES, the early higher-dose birth-control pills, cancer associated with estrogen replacement therapy, and recently toxic shock syndrome, the FDA and many doctors are extremely cautious about approving or prescribing new, potentially dangerous hormonal treatments.

However, doctors have the right to prescribe any drug (provided it is not illegal) in whatever dosage, for whatever reason they deem appropriate. So although the FDA may not approve of a substance, or the treatment for which the substance is being used, a doctor can still write out a prescription for it—and a pharmacist can choose to fill the prescription.

Most medical experts agree that progesterone therapy is still too experimental and too drastic a treatment for women with PMS. Only very rarely will no other form of treatment alleviate the symptoms. Under carefully supervised circumstances, progesterone therapy may be worth the risk to a PMS sufferer. But it should be regarded as an experimental treatment of last resort.

PMS Clinics

Up until recently, it was fairly difficult to obtain progesterone suppositories, injections, or liquids in this country. Many physicians and pharmacists were and still are hesitant to deal with unapproved drugs. And, since the FDA forbids mass production of unapproved drugs, such as progesterone, progesterone can only be compounded on a per prescription basis. But it is costly and time consuming to compound progesterone from scratch; without a large demand for the drug, most private pharmacies were not interested in compounding progesterone. Furthermore, since progesterone is a natural substance, it cannot be patented; so even large pharmaceutical companies had little interest in pursuing this venture. In addition, the FDA places restrictions on the sale of unapproved drugs, including progesterone: the finished products cannot be transported across state lines or imported from foreign countries.

On this last point, FDA officials admit it is virtually impossible to detect or stop this importation. Indeed, much of the progesterone sold to women in this country was brought in illegally from England.

But doctors and women now have a far easier time getting progesterone as a result of the opening of PMS clinics, which are mushrooming around various areas in this country.

If you suffer from PMS, the first place you might turn to is a clinic that seems to specialize in that syndrome. The PMS clinics can be very appealing to women who have never received appropriate, caring treatment from the traditional medical community. Any woman who has ever been told that her menstrual difficulties are "all in her head" would be more than grateful to go to a clinic and hear that her problems are real, they have a name, and there is a cure—progesterone.

Most women going to PMS clinics, however, are probably unaware of the experimental nature of the treatment. Indeed, they are most likely given the impression that it's been proven effective. The possible side effects are usually underplayed and some PMS clinic practitioners deny there are any ill effects associated with megadoses of progesterone. If the FDA is mentioned at all, it is usually depicted as a bunch of bureaucratic bad guys trying to prevent women from getting the treatments they need.

The owners of these PMS clinics have a very strong motivation to promote progesterone treatment—it holds an enormous potential for profit.

Almost all women who enter the clinic are diagnosed as having PMS and as requiring progesterone supplements. By the admission of one clinic proprietor, 90 percent of women who apply are accepted into therapy. The therapy, however, is extremely expensive.

Treatment includes an "introduction to PMS," which consists of a video-tape program and/or consultation with a staff member. Usually, women are given calendars on which to chart their symptoms for several months before a diagnosis is made, but sometimes the diagnosis is made on the spot. There is a routine gynecological examination and one or two counseling sessions with someone at the clinic.

How much does this cost? PMS clinics charge anywhere from $200 to $400 for their services. Blood tests, which cannot determine progesterone deficiency or the existence of PMS, are extra and can run into hundreds of dollars. And the actual treatment—the progesterone dosages—is not included in the clinic's fee. A 200 mg. suppository of progesterone can cost anywhere from $1 to $5, depending on the pharmacy that compounds the drug. Multiply that over several days or weeks each month (and some women take two, three, or more doses a day; a few women take them all month long) and the cost can become astronomical. There are women who spend thousands of dollars a year for this treatment.

Now, an internal examination by a private gynecologist averages $40 to $60, and many gynecologists will gladly discuss premenstrual symptoms with their patients as part of the office visit. It is even possible to find a private doctor who will write out prescriptions for progesterone.

So why do PMS clinics charge hundreds of dollars when essentially the same services can be had for much less?

Owners and supporters of the clinics give a threefold explanation. First, they provide emotional support for PMS sufferers that cannot be had in any other medical setting. Emotional support is a hard commodity on which to place a price tag, especially if it has been absent or denied for a long time. Perhaps it is worth the money charged. Only the individual involved can judge that.

Second, information about PMS is also provided by the clinics. But critics point out that much of the material they pass out about the syndrome is superficial, biased, and medically unsupported. The same or better information can be gleaned from any one of the dozens of magazine articles on PMS.

Third and most important, the owners of the clinics tell their patients a good percentage of the money goes to further research efforts in the field of premenstrual syndrome.

Indeed, many women who attend the clinics feel positive about contributing to efforts that will ultimately benefit themselves and other women who suffer from PMS.

But in reality, very little of this money is going to support unbiased medical or scientific research at universities or hospitals. Instead, much of it is being used to fund the production of progesterone suppositories to be sold back to women patients, or it is being used to set up new clinics or progesterone compounding pharmaceutical branches in other parts of the country. (At best, some of the fees are being applied to researching new, more pleasant ways to administer progesterone.)

As several investigative reporters and representatives of the FDA have remarked, "It is an enormous coincidence that the owners of some of these PMS clinics are also the owners of pharmaceutical concerns that manufacture progesterone."

Technically, these owners may be operating against the law. But law suits would first have to be presented and it may take years before any decision is reached.

Meanwhile, PMS can turn out to be very good business, indeed. One social worker for gynecological patients commented on this situation, "Once again, men are making a profit off of women's bodies."

Still, there are patients who believe that if anyone is profiting from progesterone treatments, it's the PMS sufferers themselves. As Ginny B., 32, a housewife, said,

> Before the PMS clinics and progesterone, I could not function. My life was falling apart. Progesterone may not be the answer, but at least now I can cope.

Ginny is not alone. Already hundreds and perhaps thousands of women have tried progesterone therapy and have become advocates of the treatment. Progesterone may or may not be the ultimate answer to PMS. But doctors and operators of these clinics hope to find out that it is.

Physicians, even many of those affiliated with PMS clinics, admit that progesterone treatment is experimental. What alarms critics of the clinics is the absence of rigorously controlled standards set by the scientific community. Dosages vary enormously, making controls essentially impossible. Women trying the drug are not carefully monitored for effects or side effects. If an individual woman has a problem and wishes to discontinue the treatment, she does so on her own. The detrimental effects are not recorded, nor is her post-progesterone progress followed.

Some women with PMS are desperate. They are deeply troubled by their monthly symptoms and are tortured with emotional or physical pain. They are vulnerable to anyone or anything that promises hope, relief, comfort, and a cure of their condition. To a degree, PMS clinics fulfill that promise. but before any woman introduces megadoses of any substance into her body, she should know the facts and the side effects of that treatment. At the PMS clinics, she will probably get only one side of the story.

Any of the pharmaceutical treatments discussed in this chapter carry risks of potential side effects and possible dangers. In most cases, these risks are tolerably small, especially if proper precautions are exercised under careful medical supervision. Women with PMS should weigh the hoped-for benefits against the chance of potential ill effects.

Again, it is important to reiterate that none of the methods suggested in this chapter are *proven* effective in alleviating premenstrual symptoms. The positive results are based on clinical and/or anecdotal observations of women who have tried the various treatments and the physicians who prescribed them. In each case, when controlled double-blind experiments have been carried out, the method of treatment ranked no better than placebos. (In one study, women rated the placebos more favorably because they didn't experience negative side effects.)

Therefore, women should consider prescription medication as a treatment for PMS with enlightened caution. Perhaps in the future, better, more effective treatments will be found and the true causes of PMS will be discovered. But until doctors and researchers know more, women are on their own.

10

LIVING WITH PREMENSTRUAL SYNDROME— SUCCESSFULLY!

It's a little easier now that I've learned more about PMS and have begun taking better care of myself. I can't say I'm cured of premenstrual syndrome, but it's definitely under control.

Janice S., 30
Management consultant

Gaining Personal Control over PMS

PMS was first identified years ago, but so far, no one has found that magical cure women have been hoping for. Perhaps one day the solution will be found. In the meantime, there is quite a bit you can do for yourself to alleviate your symptoms.

1) Identify your symptoms as related to PMS. You can overcome much frustration and self-doubt by knowing that what you are feeling is *real*.

2) Learn more about your body. In becoming more aware of and sensitive to your monthly cycle by using your chart, you can learn to predict your particular symptoms of premenstrual syndrome. Being able to predict an event already gives you more control over it. Just being able to say, "No, there is nothing seriously wrong with me. These feelings will pass in a matter of days," can help to reduce personal stress and tension.

3) Understand the various biological, psychological, and socio-logical factors involved. Knowledge is power, and power leads to control over your life. Furthermore, by learning of other women's experiences with premenstrual syndrome, you can gain assurance that you're not alone.

4) There are many self-help suggestions that can alleviate the symptoms of PMS. The best treatment for PMS may not be expensive prescription medicines or tampering with the body's hor-

mones, but rather dietary changes, exercise, and other less drastic forms of treatment. Remember, even if you do decide to try some of the new pharmaceutical methods, your treatment will be most effective if supported by sound premenstrual health management

- Eat little, but often
- Get adequate amounts of vitamins, especially vitamin B_6
- Stay away from salty foods
- Cut out caffeine
- Avoid too much alcohol
- When needed, use mild diuretic pills or natural diuretics
- Try simple analgesics for premenstrual aches and pains
- Exercise throughout your cycle—try swimming, dancing jogging, bicycling, even walking
- Enjoy your sexuality through orgasm
- Get enough rest

By adopting these ten methods, many women find relief from at least some of their symptoms within the time of one cycle. Begin now and the following premenstrual phase will probably be more comfortable and easier to bear. As the months pass by and the self-help treatments are continued, women notice their PMS phases getting easier and shorter. And as they realize they can be in control of their bodies and emotions, women gain more confidence in themselves and their ability to perform well during the time around menstruation.

It's probably difficult for most of us to change a lifetime of accustomed habit overnight. So, to make it easier on yourself, start with just one method, whatever seems most appropriate for your set of PMS symptoms. Then add on another method each cycle until you feel you have achieved desired relief.

Although most of these methods need be or should be employed only during the actual premenstrual phase, many women find they feel better all month long as a result of their improved premenstrual care. Many women have found these methods to be effective inexpensive, and safe.

5) A small percentage of women suffer from severe premenstrual pain. Medical treatment may be the only alternative. Since some

octors are not experienced in dealing with PMS or may not be
ware of the treatments available, a woman should shop to find a
uitable doctor to treat her. This may mean telephoning several
ynecologists in your area. Ask the receptionist if the doctor is
ware of PMS treatments and is he or she willing to take the time
o explore the methods with you. You may want to make an
ppointment to discuss your particular set of symptoms with the
octor before deciding to accept medical treatment. You might feel
etter and be more trusting of your judgment if your first visit to the
octor is during your symptom-free time. Since there is no sure-fire
reatment of PMS and treatments used may take several cycles
efore improvement is realized, successful therapy might involve
ollow-up office visits over a period of time. Your doctor should
lso be warm and sympathetic, and not resent giving time or
upport to a woman with premenstrual problems. Since there is no
ne pill or shot that can permanently banish PMS, doctors and
atients must work together to find a treatment that works.

Some PMS sufferers have joined together to form support groups
oncerned with premenstrual syndrome. For a contribution fee,
hey will send you a list of doctors in your state who have expe-
ience in treating PMS. Many of these doctors, though, subscribe to
he progesterone megadose theory, and may not want to try other
ess drastic methods first.

Since talking about premenstrual syndrome is one way to gain
eassurance as well as share feelings and information with other
vomen, you might want to start your own PMS club. Create a
upport group with your neighbors and friends.

Coping with Your Life During PMS Time

Once you know you have premenstrual syndrome, you can make
our life easier by following some of these guidelines:

Reduce stress on yourself

Simplify your life during PMS time. Do the major housework
vhen you are symptom-free (unless, like some women, you get the

urge to clean right at that time). Ask your husband or your childre to help in the routine tasks, cooking evening supper, washin dishes, doing the shopping. If you have two meetings, attend th more important one. Ask if the other one can be moved to nex week. If your social obligations are overwhelming, cut back o some of them until after your period. Look at your calendar. Don schedule a dinner party for 12 two days before your period i expected to start.

Prioritize—do only those tasks that are most important. Les vital tasks can be postponed. Above all, don't feel guilty if you can do all things for all people. Learn to say "no" or at least "later. You needn't tell people this is your "time of the month" or that yo have PMS, since that is, after all, a very personal matter. You'd b surprised, though, how easily most people accept a change in plan and think nothing of it.

By reducing outside stress as much as is feasible, you'll be bette equipped to cope with premenstrual changes.

Build up your physical and emotional reserves

Begin to fortify your physical reserves by taking good premen strual care of yourself. Follow the ten guidelines for PMS manage ment listed earlier in this chapter.

You can keep up your emotional reserves by having a runnin conversation with yourself. When things are upsetting, remin yourself that you may be overreacting because it's PMS time. Te yourself throughout the day that the unpleasant feelings will pas that in a few days your period will start and it will all be over. If yo must face a stressful situation, give yourself a pep talk—tell you self that you will do well, that you will succeed even though it i "that time of the month." (Keep in mind those studies that sho women do just as well right before their period as they do at an other time of the cycle.) Always remember that as bad as you ma feel inside, it probably doesn't show on the outside. The truth i most people are too involved in their own lives to perceive you subtle shifts of mood. And when it comes right down to it, no on can really tell when a woman is premenstrual, menstrual, or post-menstrual unless she tells you. To prove it, observe the next woman who passes by. Can you tell what phase she is in?

You'd be surprised how a little psychic encouragement on your part will give you the extra confidence you may need premenstrually. As you learn that you can cope before your period, you'll probably find you have greater self-assurance throughout the month.

Organize your life to take into account those PMS days

Whatever may be said about PMS, it is *predictable*. You can chart when your next bout with premenstrual symptoms will begin and can be assured when it will end. This is the beginning of control. By knowing when it will start, you can organize your life to take into account those PMS days.

Start by reducing the stress in your life. With your calendar in front of you, put a little thought and planning to everything you do. Rearrange schedules if necessary. Move a deadline up a week. Finish important projects before your premenstrual phase begins. Postpone not-so-important tasks. Then during your PMS days, schedule enough time to relax, to recoup, to rediscover your personal equilibrium.

Do some little things for yourself, such as:

- Take a long, hot bath.
- Ease body tension and stiffness with a heating pad.
- Wrap yourself in an electric blanket.
- Get a massage from your partner or a professional masseuse.
- Massage your own aching, cramped muscles with a deep heating oil or cream.
- Sip a cup of hot herbal tea.
- Take your mind off your symptoms by going out to a movie or a play.
- Relax in bed with a good book. (In fact, why not read books

that can help you overcome particular PMS symptoms? Read cookbooks for low-salt meals, diet books for people with low blood sugar, self-help books on coping with back-ache, headache, anxiety, or depression.)

Telling the Important People in Your Life about PMS

Premenstrual syndrome most directly affects you. But it can also affect other important people in your life, especially those who love you.

Talking to Your Partner

Sometimes, the man in your life may recognize your premen-strual symptoms and link them to your menstrual cycles before you do. But other times he may be confused and disturbed by changes he sees in you, but cannot identify.

It's important that husbands and wives (or live-in partners) discuss premenstrual syndrome. Many men know very little of what women go through each cycle. Some men may even fear the mysterious mood swings, physical changes, the pain women expe-rience as part of their menstrual cycle. It can stir up early learned associations that may be unpleasant and disturbing. A man needs to be reassured that there are medical reasons why PMS occurs, that millions of women experience it, and that his woman is not men-tally ill or abnormal. Share this book with him. He may gain a better insight and understanding of the condition.

Unfortunately, not all men respond positively to information about PMS. Some men turn the situation into a power play. He may want to use PMS to assert his superiority over the woman. Some want to put the wife in the "sick role." It's not always verbalized, but the underlying dynamic is clear: "Aha, I knew there was something wrong with you. You cannot control yourself and therefore can't be trusted with the checkbook/ the children/ making decisions. I'll be in charge from now on. I'll keep you under control."

On the other hand, once men know about PMS, many are eager to support their partners in their attempts to overcome the symptoms. Some join their wives in a week of low-salt dinners. Others make sure their partners eat every four hours. Some help give their women a little extra will power to stick to their premenstrual management program. Many are agreeable to changing plans or remind their partners not to overdo work or social commitments that week. And when women are relaxed and refreshed enough to enjoy their heightened sexuality during that time, their men can even look forward to the premenstrual phase!

It's very important that a woman let her man know she's taking steps to overcome her symptoms and that she is in control of herself during that time. This will reassure her partner if he is uneasy about things related to menstruation and may also prevent a power-play situation from developing.

But if you are feeling sad or edgy or anxious, if you have aches and pains, it's perfectly reasonable to share those feelings too with your partner, so he can understand your moods in context and provide the emotional support you probably can use during your premenstrual time.

Explaining PMS to Your Children

It's important that mothers share with their children how they are feeling, whether or not they decide to explain it as a manifestation of premenstrual changes. The reason children should know what their mothers are experiencing is that (1) they probably sense your pain and your moods without your having to tell them, and (2) when they don't know the reason, children often blame themselves for things that happen to their parents. This can be troublesome to a developing child.

Some mothers feel comfortable about telling their children about PMS, especially if the mothers are open about discussions of menstruation and the inevitable questions about reproduction and sexuality. Some women feel all right about talking to their daughters, especially if they are already past pubescence, but feel uneasy about talking to their sons. Other mothers are quite frank about their condition and feel it's best to explain it to both their sons and their daughters of any age.

On the other hand, some women do not want to tell their children about PMS specifically because they may be uneasy discussing such a private matter with their children. Others don't want to give inadvertently the impression that PMS is a disease, resulting in the children's worrying that "Mommy's sick." Still others don't want their children to grow up with negative associations about the menstrual cycle. Some mothers prefer to wait until their daughters are in their teens to explain PMS in such a way that they can learn how to manage their symptoms should they occur in the future.

This is a highly personal decision, to be made by each woman in consideration of her own unique needs and circumstances.

Whether or not you relate it to PMS, it's probably better to tell your children when you are down, or on edge, or feeling achy. They can then begin to understand your moods or behavior, know it's not their fault, and feel secure in your love.

Meanwhile, keep up your diet and rest plans. If you need to, arrange for a sitter to take your children out for a couple of hours while you soothe jangled nerves by relaxing in a hot bath or taking a much needed nap. Ask a neighbor to watch your children for a while. Perhaps your husband can take over some of the daily chores. Get your children to become involved in household tasks— children need to feel needed as much as they need to feel loved.

Talking with Other Women

One of the worst parts of PMS is keeping all your emotions inside, fearing there is something wrong with you. But one of the best therapies for PMS is talking about it to other women. Almost every woman has it to some degree, so the chances are high you'll find someone to share your experiences with. Most women feel enormously relieved to express their feelings and to learn they are not alone.

This is one aspect of the therapeutic nature of talking about PMS to women friends. The other aspect is very practical. Through the ages, women have discovered for themselves ways to cope with their premenstrual symptoms and these can be shared between women. You might get some new ideas and renewed hope and encouragement to overcome PMS.

Should You Tell Your Boss?

Premenstrual syndrome is a very personal condition that many women instinctively feel is not to be discussed on the job. Some prefer not to reveal intimate parts of their lives to co-workers and employers. Others sense that such information could be turned against them.

It happened to Barbara M., 35, an assistant sales manager at a large pharmaceutical firm.

> *Encouraged by a PMS clinic nurse to tell people about my condition, I told my boss that I have PMS and may not be up to par in my work during that time. I expected him to sympathize; after all, we work in a company that specializes in health and medical products. But he didn't. He just stared at me and then said, "Miss M., that is a highly unprofessional attitude." I knew at once I made a terrible mistake. Now I sincerely doubt he's going to consider me for promotion.*

Women should be cautious in telling others at work of their bouts with PMS. It's not a matter of sex discrimination. Barbara's boss would probably have reacted the same way if a man had told him "I get migraines every so often and can't always do my best" or "I've got back trouble so don't expect me to always get the job done."

Nor would it have mattered if Barbara's boss had been a woman. Most women have some degree of premenstrual syndrome, painful menstrual cramps, or both, and manage to be productive at work. They may very well be unsympathetic to another woman who says she can't fulfill her work obligations during that time.

In general, it is best to keep your personal ailments separate from your work commitments. But if you must talk about your premenstrual symptoms, try to convey the information that you are taking steps to overcome it and that you are in control. In fact, if you can show how your learning to cope has benefited you when it comes to handling deadlines or difficult situations at work, you might be able to turn PMS into a plus!

For too long, the existence of premenstrual syndrome has been unrecognized, ridiculed, or rebutted. There still is a strong resistance to discussing anything concerning the menstrual cycle.

But fortunately times are changing and women are helping to change the times. No longer do women have to believe that their bodily functions keep them from being or doing whatever is humanly desired and possible. No longer do women have to think they are "sick" or "cursed" or "out of control" before or during menstruation. Nor do we have to hear that the premenstrual aches, pains, and emotional changes are imaginary.

We now know that PMS is real and women do not have to suffer. We can take control of this part of our lives. The cure for PMS has yet to be discovered, but by learning of the treatments and techniques now available and by gaining strength from self-knowledge, we can survive premenstrual syndrome—successfully!

PMS AND MEN

The aches and pains of PMS may seem to be the domain of women. But the truth is, men sometimes feel irritable, depressed, or out-of-sorts. They have backaches, joint pain, bouts with constipation and diarrhea, and can't always attribute their symptoms to something specific. Men have "down days" as do all human beings. In fact, when you reconsider the 70 or so symptoms listed in chapter 2, you realize that, except for a few sex-specific complaints, men can and do experience any of these "PMS" symptoms.

Some men even suspect that their individual "down phases" come in cycles.

In the course of researching and writing this book, I came across several men who revealed personal observations and reflections they would probably be reluctant to share with another man.

After a lengthy interview with an executive at a major pharmaceutical company about the symptoms and treatment of PMS, the conversation turned to his experience.

> *Every so often, I get this craving for chocolates and sweets, which is odd, because I don't usually have a sweet tooth. I actually timed these cravings once and they came just about every 31-32 days. I wonder what causes that?*

Then recovering from his slight embarrassment, he joked,

> *Maybe I have PMS and don't know it!*
>
> Robert T., 42

Some time later, I had lunch with a friend who is a playwright. We talked about his soon-to-be-produced musical and, of course, about my work on this book. Halfway through the second glass of wine, he confided,

> *Sometimes, I feel like crying for no reason at all. It just comes over me and I have to get away from people then because I don't want them to see me with tears in my eyes. They'd think I was crazy. It happens every couple of weeks or so. I know when women go through it, they can look at a calendar and say "Oh, it's PMS." But what do I have? How am I supposed to explain this?*
>
> Joel C., 28

Other men probably notice various "symptoms" that happen every so often that they can't pin down to any outside event. Some men may even have "sympathetic PMS."

> *Once a month, just before my wife gets her period, I get something like what she must be going through. I feel waterlogged and irritable. I get joint pain and my muscles feel tight. I have to check with her to see if it's that time, otherwise I'd think something was wrong with me. To tell you the truth, I think I get PMS worse than she does.*
>
> David M., 30
> Salesman

Even "macho-men" may have something similar. I mentioned the subject to a muscled truck driver who, perhaps, summed up the phenomenon,

When I get into one of those phases, I tell my girlfriend, "Don't bother me, I'm getting my comma." Women get their periods. Men get their commas.

Charlie S., 34

Very few studies have been carried out to determine if men experience cyclicity in their emotions or physical experiences. Some recent investigations though, have indicated men appear to have temperature cycles that occur every seventeen to thirty-five days depending on the individual. This seems remarkably coincidental to the time period of women's menstrual cycles. Furthermore, it seems that men who live with and are emotionally close to their wife or girl friend have temperature cycles that track their woman's monthly temperature cycle. To date, there is no scientific explanation for this change or its cause.

It is known that men also have hormonal fluctuations, although not as pronounced as in women. For example, testosterone levels rise in the early morning and fall as the day progresses. Even the seasons affect testosterone levels. Studies in Europe show the hormone peaks in October.

Although there is little current interest in studying these cycles or cycles in men's behavior and moods, this topic will probably make for some fascinating research sometime in the future.

In the meantime, perhaps what knowledge we do have can serve to strengthen the natural ties between men and women. Rather than forever battling each other over the question of hormones, we might be able to recognize our common humanness and provide one another with understanding, compassion, and kindness during whatever period or comma we're going through.

PMS UPDATE

The good news carries on—never again should women be told PMS is just an imaginary female problem. Premenstrual syndrome is a very real physical phenomenon that millions of women experience every month. As of this writing in January 1984, there is hope, there is help, and there are exciting new developments in the treatment of PMS that every woman should know about.

New PMS Clinics

There are now approximately 175 PMS clinics across the country. Although most encourage the use of the hormone progesterone, a few clinics have opened recently that prefer the natural approach to PMS management.

Two excellent centers for counseling, treatments advice, and referrals, are:

Women's Research and Treatment Center
Amherst Plaza Professional Building
131 Route 101A
Amherst, NH 03031
Contact: Bonnie Jensen Oas, R.N., Director
(603) 889-0070

Premenstrual Research Foundation
Box 14574
Las Vegas, NV 89114
Contact: Lee Horner, Director

The Vitamin B-6 Scare

Vitamin B-6 (pyridoxine hydrochloride) is often used by women to overcome premenstrual symptoms such as depression, bloating, fatigue, irritability, agitation, and general feelings of tension. Recommended supplements are 50-200 mg. a day. Some doctors suggest up to 800 mg. a day be used during the premenstrual phase. But as success of this treatment became more widely known, some people figured that "more must be better" and began taking huge doses of 2-6 grams (2000-6000 mg.) a day. Doctors warn that too much vitamin B-6 can result in sensory nerve disorders symptomized by numbness and loss of sensation. It is believed that megadoses of the vitamin flood the system and kill nerve cells. There have been a few reports of such crippling effects that victims can no longer lift anything or can barely walk. Fortunately, in most cases, patients improve after they stop taking the vitamin.

Unfortunately, this "vitamin scare" was widely publicized and scared many women from taking any B-6 at all.

Vitamin B-6 in reasonable doses is an important factor in overcoming PMS. In the 1970s researchers confirmed the beneficial effect of vitamin B-6 upon depression in women using oral contraception and in those experiencing PMS symptoms.

Scientists are now forging yet another link between the lack of B-6 and depression. It seems that B-6 is essential to the production of certain brain neurotransmitters, in particular dopamine and serotonin, which are known to regulate mood. Vitamin B-6 may play an essential role in boosting those brain chemicals providing sufferers a premenstrual emotional boost.

B-6 is found naturally in beef liver, brewer's yeast, wheat germ, brown rice, green leafy vegetables, and sweet potatoes. Vitamin supplements of B-6 should be taken in a combination pill with other B-complex vitamins, because the body can best absorb and utilize B-6 when other B vitamins are present.

Many people assume vitamins in any amount are 100 percent safe, but vitamin megadosing can be harmful. Women with PMS should be aware of what kind of vitamins and how much they are taking. If there are any troubling side effects, vitamin supplements should be reported to the doctor along with any medications.

Oil of Evening Primrose

Oil of evening primrose has recently received a flurry of publicity as a newly discovered cure for premenstrual syndrome.

The oil from the evening primrose flower is rich in gamma-linolenic acid. Although medical researchers do not know precisely how (and whether) evening primrose oil is responsible for easing PMS symptoms, there are two leading theories.

First, it is known that this substance is essential for the body's production of one type of prostaglandin (a hormonelike chemical) suspected of playing a role in physical PMS symptoms. It is thought that oil of evening primrose acts with this prostaglandin, thereby reducing premenstrual problems.

Second, some recent research suggests that oil of evening primrose may actually be effective because of the way it interacts with prolactin (a reproductive hormone). Prolactin production is thought by some researchers to be a major PMS culprit.

Experiments in England show that oil of evening primrose is very effective in supressing PMS symptoms in women who have not found relief from other treatments; however, science has yet to firmly prove its effectiveness over a placebo or other forms of natural remedies. Oil of evening primrose is not a "cure," but it may be worth a try.

Oil of evening primrose can be found in health food stores but is rather expensive. One week's supply can range from $4.00 to $10.00.

PMS Vitamin Formulas

A few health-food/vitamin companies have introduced products specially formulated for PMS sufferers.

In essence, these are tablets that contain a combination of vitamins and minerals frequently recommended to combat premenstrual syndrome. These vitamin pills usually include calcium, magnesium, B-6, potassium, and folic acid. Some also add dandelion, parsley, and watercress, which act as mild diuretics.

These PMS vitamin formulas are basically beneficial, provided they are not abused by taking large doses. But since they are "new" and "specially formulated," they may be more costly than a multivitamin with the same ingredients manufactured for the general public. Compare ingredients and prices.

New Over-the-Counter Medication

In September 1983, the first over-the-counter medication specifically positioned for PMS was introduced to the national market. It's called "Premesyn PMS" and is manufactured by Chattem Consumer Products, a division of Chattem, Inc.

Premesyn PMS contains acetaminophen, pamabrom, and pyrilamine maleate. It is aspirin and caffeine free. The capsules are formulated to relieve premenstrual uterine cramping and general bodily malaise, as well as to reduce feelings of irritability and tension. They also work as a mild diuretic to reduce water gain that results in uncomfortable bloating. Water retention is associated with premenstrual mood swings and headaches.

Based on clinical tests, a panel of medical experts appointed by the FDA have concluded that the combination of drugs used in Premesyn PMS is safe and effective in relieving mild to moderate premenstrual discomfort.

Used in conjunction with dietary changes and an exercise program, Premesyn PMS might well be one of the first lines of defense to use against premenstrual syndrome. In general, milder

elf-help forms of treatment should be tried before resorting to
prescription drugs or hormonal therapy.

Premesyn PMS can be purchased at major drug stores and
supermarkets.

The Yeast Connection

Some doctors have theorized that the yeast germ, candida albe-
ans, may be an underlying problem for many women with PMS
symptoms. Although the yeast normally lives on mucous membranes, certain factors such as taking antibiotics or birth control
pills, douching, a high carbohydrate diet, having diabetes, and
pregnancy can cause candida to flourish out of control, resulting in
vaginitis, mouth infections, and skin rashes. New discoveries show
that the yeast also produces toxins that can cause recurring PMS-
like symptoms such as uterine cramping, headaches, fatigue, irritability, and depression. Although there is little hard evidence to
support this theory, doctors who subscribe to it recommend a
sound, balanced diet, low in yeast-containing foods, and nutritional supplements of zinc, vitamin B-6, and oil of evening primrose. Anti-yeast medications may also be prescribed.

An abundance of yeast can be added to the long list of possible
causes of PMS. In general, the "cure" is safe enough, and the
recommended diet is basically wholesome and healthy.

Progesterone Therapy

The controversy continues. Some doctors maintain that hormone supplements are the preferred treatment for PMS. In general
though, most of the gynecological health care community are
cautious and skeptical about its use. There is virtually no evidence
to support the theory that women with PMS have a progesterone
deficiency warranting supplementation.

Most seriously, it is now known that almost all women using
progesterone will experience changes in their normal menstrual

cycle. It is thought that this interruption of the normal cycle is wh
premenstrual symptoms seem to abate.

Doctors and clinicians who oppose progesterone use are cor
cerned about its long-term effects, which are unknown but a
suspected to cause cardiovascular disease and cancer.

They also point out that they see the same success rate fro
milder forms of treatment, such as dietary, exercise, and attitudin.
changes, as well as judicious use of symptomatic medication.

It is unlikely that the Food and Drug Administration will san
tion megadoses of progesterone for treatment of PMS. Progesteror
therapy is just too drastic and too risky for the vast majority
women. Under pressure from pro-progesterone advocates, the FD
has approved two scientific experiments at Duke University and
the National Institute of Health to test for absorption rates ar
efficacy.

The duration and doses will probably be criticized by advocat
as being too little and too low. Nonetheless, the results will
eagerly awaited by doctors and patients alike.

PMS remains a medical mystery. It eludes quick, complete reli
In spite of hopeful promises, there is no known effective and sa
pharmacological treatment of the condition. There is still
answer to PMS that will work for all women. There are, howev
many different types of relief available, from self-help to over-th
counter medications and prescription drugs, to counseling a
attudinal changes. All have been described in this book.

Which will work best? Well, we are still on our own. The on
way to find out which treatment or combination of treatmer
works best is simply to try those suggested here for specific sym
toms and evaluate them objectively according to which seems m
effective.

Glossary

ANALGESIC—Any drug or agent that relieves pain.

ANOVULATORY CYCLE—A menstrual cycle in which ovulation does not occur.

ANTICOAGULANT—Any agent or drug that prevents or reduces the clotting of blood.

BIOPSY—Surgical removal, or excision, of living tissue for the purpose of examination or diagnosis.

CERVIX—The neck of the uterus, located at the lower end of the uterus. The cervix forms a passageway from the uterus to the vagina.

CLITORIS—The small organ composed of erectile tissue, situated in the vulva area. The clitoris has numerous sensitive nerve endings and is the center of sexual sensations in the female reproductive system.

CONGESTIVE DYSMENORRHEA—A variety of symptoms that may include lower abdomen pain, water retention, constipation, nausea, altered appetite, breast tenderness, joint pain, headaches, fatigue, lethargy, anxiety, tension, depression, among others, which are experienced prior to the onset of menstruation. Congestive dysmenorrhea is another name for premenstrual syndrome.

CORPUS LUTEUM—A yellowish body located in the ovary that develops from the ruptured Graafian follicle after ovulation. The corpus luteum manufactures and secretes estrogen and progesterone, which prepares the lining of the uterus for possible implantation of the fertilized egg. If pregnancy does not occur, the corpus luteum degenerates, causing progesterone levels to fall, which precipitates the onset of menstruation.

CYST—A membranous sac filled with fluid or semisolid matter.

DILATION AND CURETTAGE (D & C)—A surgical procedure whereby the cervical canal is widened, or dilated, and the uterine cavity is gently scraped by use of a long, thin-handled instrument with a small, spoon-shaped loop on the end, called the curette. A D & C is often performed as a diagnostic technique and/or to treat certain menstrual disorders.

DIURETIC—Any agent or drug that increases the amount of urine processed by the kidneys. Diuretics are used to prevent or lessen the accumulation of fluids in the body.

DYSMENORRHEA—A general term for pain or discomfort associated with menstruation. (See congestive d., secondary d., spasmodic d.)

EDEMA—Excessive or abnormal accumulation of fluid in body tissues, resulting in swelling or weight gain.

ENDOCRINE GLAND—A ductless gland that secretes hormones. The major endocrine glands of the body include pituitary, thyroid, parathyroids, thymus, adrenals, pancreas, testes, and ovaries.

ENDOMETRIOSIS—The presence of tissue fragments normally found in the lining of the uterus, or endometrium, in abnormal sites such as the ovaries, Fallopian tubes, bladder, or outside of the uterus. May cause pain, menstrual difficulties, or sterility if left untreated.

ENDOMETRIUM—The lining of the uterus, rich in blood and special glands to support a fertilized egg. This lining is shed once per menstrual cycle if no pregnancy occurs.

ESTROGEN—Considered the major female sex hormone, secreted by the ovarian follicles and by the corpus luteum. Estrogen promotes the development and maintenance of the reproductive and sexual organs, the secondary female sexual characteristics, and contributes to the control of the menstrual cycle.

FALLOPIAN TUBE. One of two funnel-shaped tubes on each side of the upper uterus, connecting each ovary to the uterus. Once per cycle, the matured, released egg is conveyed through the tube into the uterus. Also called oviduct.

FIBROUS—Having the characteristic of threadlike structures.

GRAAFIAN FOLLICLE—A minute sac containing the maturing ovum. At ovulation, the sac bursts, releasing the matured ovum. The empty follicle is then transformed into the corpus luteum, which secretes progesterone and estrogen.

HORMONE—Specific chemical substance produced by an endo-crine gland. Hormones are secreted into the bloodstream to regulate or activate various physical processes of tissues and organs.

HYPOGLYCEMIA—Decreased levels of or a deficiency of sugar in the blood.

HYPOTHALAMUS—The part of the brain below the cerebrum, closest to the pituitary. The hypothalamus controls the central nervous system, regulates ovulation, and aids in the function of other organs and systems of the body.

INSULIN—A hormone secreted by the pancreas that regulates blood-sugar levels.

MENARCHE—The first menstrual period.

MENSES—The menstrual flow, or menstruation.

MENSTRUAL CYCLE—The cyclical chain of events occurring in the female reproductive organs. The cycle averages 26 to 32 days and is marked by the onset of menstrual bleeding. The menstrual cycle is controlled by hormones from the pituitary gland and the ovaries.

MENSTRUATION—The normal cyclical flow of blood, actually the endometrial lining, from the uterus through the cervical opening and out the vagina. Menstruation usually lasts three to seven days and occurs approximately once a month, commenc-ing between the ages of 9 and 14 and ceasing between the ages of 45 and 55.

MITTELSCHMERTZ—Abdominal pain or discomfort exper-ienced by some women at the time of ovulation.

OVA—The female reproduction cells, or eggs, which are devel-oped in the ovaries (see ovum).

OVARY—One of two small paired oval-shaped bodies located on each side of the uterus and connected to it by ligaments and membranes. The ovaries develop the eggs, or ova, as well as manufacture estrogen and progesterone. ·

OVULATION—The moment when the Graafian follicle rup-tures, releasing the matured egg from the wall of the ovary.

OVUM—The female egg cell, developed in the ovary. Usually one ovum matures per menstrual cycle.

PARAMENSTRUUM—The period of time before the onset of menstruation and the days of menstruation.

PITUITARY GLAND—A small oval endocrine gland, functioning under the hypothalamus and lying in the base of the brain. The pituitary secretes several hormones including FSH and LH, which aid in the regulation of the menstrual cycle. The pituitary is often termed the "master gland" as it regulates and/or affects all other endocrine glands and hormones in the body.

PLACEBO—A harmless substance having no active ingredient, administered as a medicine for psychological benefit or in experimental research. In a "double blind" test, neither the physician nor the patient knows whether a placebo or the medicine was given. Also called a sugar pill.

PREMENSTRUUM—The period of time, variously defined as 4 to 14 days, before the onset of menstruation.

PROGESTERONE—An ovarian hormone secreted by the corpus luteum. Progesterone's primary function is to thicken the uterine lining and ready the various support systems to maintain a pregnancy.

PROGESTOGENS (PROGESTAGENS, PROGESTINS)—Synthetically produced substances that act like progesterone. Progestogens are often used in the treatment of various menstrual problems and are one of the components in birth-control pills.

PROSTAGLANDINS—Hormone-like substances found in almost all body tissues. Prostaglandins are essential to numerous body functions, including the contraction of smooth muscle organs such as the uterus. The full effect and characteristics of prostaglandins are still being discovered and researched.

PROSTAGLANDIN-INHIBITING DRUG (ANTI-PROSTAGLANDINS)—Any drug that reduces the amount of or prevents the production of prostaglandins in the body.

PSYCHOGENIC—Originating from the psyche, or mind.

PSYCHOSOMATIC—Describes condition that is both physiological and psychological.

SECONDARY DYSMENORRHEA—Menstrual pain caused by physiological disease, disorder, or abnormality.

Glossary

SPASMODIC DYSMENORRHEA—Localized pain felt in the uterus or lower abdomen, and sometimes in the lower back, buttocks, inner parts of upper thighs, and/or genitals, during the first day or two of menstrual bleeding. The pain is experienced as dull or acute spasms or cramping.

UTERUS—A pear-shaped hollow muscular organ located in the lower abdomen. The fertilized ovum is implanted in the uterus, where it develops. The uterine muscles contract to expel the fetus during labor and aid in the expulsion of the endometrial lining, or menstrual blood, during menstruation. Also called the womb.

VAGINA—The muscular tube extending from one end of the cervix to the opening of the vulva, or the external female genitals. It is through the vagina that the menstrual flow is passed from the body. Also called the birth canal.

VASOCONSTRICTORS—Any agent or drug that causes the blood vessels to narrow.

Bibliography

Abplanalp, J. M., Donnelly, A. F., Rose, R. M., "Psychoendocrinology of the Menstrual Cycle: Enjoyment of Daily Activities & Moods." *Psychosomatic Medicine*, 1, 1979.

Abraham, G. and Hargrove, J. T., "Effect of Vitamin B6 Supplement on Premenstrual Syndrome." *Infertility*, 3, 1980.

Andersch, B., Hahn, L., Anderson, M., and Isaksson, B., "Body Water and Weight in Patients with Premenstrual Tension." *British Medical Journal of Obstetrics and Gynaecology*, 85 July, 1978.

Angier, Natalie, "Dr. Jekyll and Ms. Hyde." *Discover*, November 1982.

Allen, Jennifer, "Pre-Menstrual Frenzy." *New York*, November 1, 1982.

Asso, D., "Levels of Arousal in the Premenstrual Phase." *British Journal of Social Clinical Psychology*, 17, 1978.

Berry, C., and McGuire, F. L., "Menstrual Distress and Acceptance of Sexual Role." *American Journal of Obstetrics and Gynecology*, 114, 1972.

Boffey, Philip M., "Psychiatric Group Urges Stiffer Rules for Insanity Plea." *The New York Times*, January 20, 1983.

Brahams, Diana, "Medicine and the Law." *Lancet*, November 28, 1981.

Brody, Jane E., "Menstruation." *The New York Times*, May 24, 1978.

Bry, Adelaide, "It Terrifies Me to Discover I Can Be That Violent." *New Woman*, December, 1982.

Budoff, Penny Wise, *No More Menstrual Cramps and Other Good News*. Penguin Books, 1981.

_____. "Treatment of Dysmenorrhea." *American Journal of Obstetrics and Gynecology*, 129, September 15, 1977.

_____. "Use of Mefanamic Acid in the Treatment of Primary Dysmenorrhea." *Journal of the American Medical Association*, 241, 1979.

Carroll, Bernard J., and Steiner, Meir, "The Psychobiology of Premenstrual Dysphoria: The Role of Prolactins." *Psychoneuroendocrinology*, 3, 1978.

Chan, W. Y., Dawood, M. Y., and Fuchs, F., "Prostaglandins in Primary Dysmenorrhea—Comparison of Prophylactic and Nonprophylactic Treatment with Ibuprofen and the Use of Oral Contraceptive." *American Journal of Medicine*, March 1981.

Check, J. H., "Emotional Aspects of Menstrual Dysfunction." *Psychosomatic Medicine*, 19, 1978.

Dalton, Katharina, "Effect of Menstruation on Schoolgirls' Weekly Work."*British Medical Journal*, 1, 1960.

———. "Menstruation and Accidents." *British Medical Journal*, 2, 1960.

———. *Once a Month*. Hunter House, 1979.

———. *Premenstrual Syndrome*. Pantheon Book, 1973.

———. *Premenstrual Syndrome and Progesterone Therapy*. Year Book Medical Publishers, 1977.

Dan, A., Graham, E., and Brecher, C. (eds.), *Menstrual Cycle: A Synthesis of Interdisciplinary Research*. Springer, 1980.

Delaney, J., Lupton, M. J., and Toth, E., *The Curse: A Cultural History of Menstruation*. E. P. Dalton, 1976.

Deutsch, Helene, *The Psychology of Women: A Psychoanalytic Interpretation*. Grune & Stratton, 1944.

Edmiston, Susan, "Now Premenstrual Syndrome Emerges as Important Issue." *The New York Times*, July 22, 1982.

Fields, Steffi, "Crime and Premenstrual Tension." *People*, April 5, 1982.

Frank, Robert T., "The Hormonal Causes of Premenstrual Tension." *Archives of Neurology and Psychiatry*, 26, 1931.

Friedman, Richard C. (ed.), *Behavior and The Menstrual Cycle*. Marcel Dekker, Inc., 1982.

Golub, Sharon, "The Effect of Premenstrual Anxiety and Depression on Cognitive Function." *Journal of Personality and Social Psychology*, 34, 1976.

———. "The Magnitude of Premenstrual Anxiety and Depression." *Psychosomatic Medicine*, 38, 1976.

Golub, Sharon, and Harrington, Denise Murphy, "Premenstrual

and Menstrual Mood Changes in Adolescent Women." *Journal of Personality and Social Psychology*, 41, 1981.

Haney, Daniel Q., "Report Raps Emphasis on Breast Ills." *The News-Journal Papers*, October 15, 1982.

Harding, M. Esther, *The Way of All Women*. Harper & Row, Publishers, Inc., 1970.

————. *Woman's Mysteries*. Bantam Books, 1973.

Henig, R., "Dispelling Menstrual Myths." *The New York Times Magazine*, March 7, 1982.

Herrmann, W. M., and Beach, R. C., "Experimental and Clinical Data Indicating the Psychotropic Properties of Progestogens." *Postgraduate Medical Journal*, 54, supplement 2, 1978.

Hoffman, Jerome J., "A Double-Blind Crossover Clinical Trial of an OTC Diuretic in the Treatment of Premenstrual Tension and Weight Gain." *Current Therapeutic Research*, November, 1979.

Hongladarom, Gail Chapman, and others, *The Complete Book of Women's Health*. Prentice-Hall, 1982.

Jones, B. M., Jones, M. K., and Hatcher, E. M., "Cognitive Deficits in Women Alcoholics as a Function of Gynecological Status." *Journal of Studies of Alcohol*, 41, 1980.

Keiffer, E., "Premenstrual Syndrome." *Family Circle*, April 6, 1982.

Kintzing, Jennifer, "Menstrual Signals: What They Reveal About You at What Age." *Self*, November 1982.

Kinch, Robert A. H., "Help for Patients with Premenstrual Tension." *Consultant*, April 1979.

Kyger, K., and Webb, W. W., "Progesterone Levels and Psychological State in Normal Women." *American Journal of Obstetrics and Gynecology*, 713, 1972.

Labrum, Anthony H., "Prolactin and Premenstrual Syndrome." *Female Patient*, July 1979.

Lauersen, Niels, and Whitney, Steven, *It's Your Body: A Woman's Guide to Gynecology*. Grosset & Dunlap, 1977.

Lauersen, Niels, with Stukane, Eileen, *Listen to Your Body: A Gynecologist Answers a Woman's Most Intimate Questions*. Fireside/Simon & Schuster, 1982.

Lennane, K. Jean, and Lennane, R. John, "Alleged Psychogenic

Disorders in Women—A Possible Manifestation of Sexual Prejudice." *New England Journal of Medicine*, 288, February 1973.

Lever, Judy, with Brush, Michael G., *Pre-Menstrual Tension*. Bantam Books, 1982.

Long, James W., *The Essential Guide to Prescription Drugs*. Harper & Row, Publishers, Inc., 1982.

Love, Susan M., "Fibrocystic Breast Disease." *New England Journal of Medicine*, October 15, 1982.

Madaras, Lynda, and Patterson, Jane, with Schick, Peter, *Womancare: A Gynecological Guide to Your Body*. Avon Books 1981.

Maddux, Hilary C., *Menstruation*. Banbury Books, Inc., 1981.

Masters, William H., and Johnson, Virginia, *Human Sexual Response*. Little, Brown & Co., 1966.

Money, John, and Ehrhardt, A. A., *Man, Woman, Boy, Girl*. Johns Hopkins University Press, 1972.

Moos, R., "The Development of a Menstrual Distress Questionnaire." *Psychosomatic Medicine*, 30, 1968.

———. "Menstrual Distress Questionnaire Manual." Social Ecology Laboratory, Dept. of Psychiatry, Stanford University, 1976.

Morton, J. H., "Premenstrual Tension," *American Journal of Obstetrics and Gynecology*, 60, 1950.

Nolen, William A., "So You Think You Have Low Blood Sugar." *McCall's*, September 1982.

Novah, A. B. and Edmund R., *Novah's Textbook of Gynecology*. The Williams & Wilkins Co., 1970.

Paige, Karen, "Women Learn to Sing the Menstrual Blues." *Psychology Today*, September 1973.

Parlee, Mary Brown, "The Premenstrual Syndrome." *Psychology Bulletin*, December 1973.

Parsons, Langdon, and Sommers, Sheldon C., *Gynecology*. 2nd ed., W. B. Saunders, 1978.

Paxton, Mary Jean Wallace, *The Female Body in Control*. Prentice-Hall, Inc., 1981.

Pickles, V. R., "Prostaglandins and Aspirin." *Nature*, September 1, 1972.

Bibliography

"PMS and You," National Center for Premenstrual Syndrome & Menstrual Distress, 1982.

"Raging Hormones," *The New York Times*, January 11, 1982.

Reid, R. L., "Premenstrual Syndrome: A Therapeutic Enigma." *Drug Therapy*, April 1982.

Reid, R. W., and Yen, S.S.C., "Premenstrual Syndrome." *Journal of Obstetrics and Gynecology*, 139, 1981.

Rinzler, Carol Ann, *Strictly Female: An Evaluation of Brand-Name Health and Hygiene Products for Women*. Plume/ The New American Library, Inc., 1981.

Rodin, J., "Menstruation, Reattribution and Competence." *Journal of Personality and Social Psychology*, 33, 1976.

Ruble, Diane N., "Premenstrual Symptoms: A Reinterpretation." *Science*, 197, July 15, 1977.

Sanders, Lawrence, *The Third Deadly Sin*. Berkley Books, 1981.

Sampson, Gwyneth A., "Premenstrual Syndrome: A Double-Blind Controlled Trial of Progesterone and Placebo." *British Journal of Psychiatry*, 135, 1979.

Schrotenboer, Kathryn, and Subak-Sharpe, Genell J., *Freedom from Menstrual Cramps*. Simon & Schuster, 1981.

Schwartz, A., Zor, U., Lindner, H. R., and Naor, S., "Primary Dysmenorrhea." *American Journal of Obstetrics and Gynecology*, November 1974.

Silber, Sherman J., *The Male: A Comprehensive Guide to the Male Sexual System*. Charles Scribner's Sons, 1981.

Silbergeld, S., Brast, N., and Noble, E. P., "The Menstrual Cycle: A Double-Blind Study of Symptoms, Mood and Behavior, and Biochemical Variables." *Psychosomatic Medicine*, 33, 1971.

Sommer, Barbara, "The Effect of Menstruation on Cognitive and Perceptual Motor Behavior: A Review." *Psychosomatic Medicine*, 35, 1973.

_____. "How Does Menstruation Affect Cognitive Competence and Psychophysiological Response?" To be published in *Women and Health*.

_____. "Menstrual Cycle Changes and Intellectual Performance." *Psychosomatic Medicine*, 34, 1972.

————. "Stress and Menstrual Distress." *Journal of Human Stress*, 4, 1978.

Spiroff, Leon, Glass, Robert H., and Kase, Nathan G., *Clinical Gynecologic Endocrinology and Infertility*. The Williams & Wilkins Co., 1978.

Steiner, M., and Carroll, B. J., "The Psychobiology of Premenstrual Dysphoria: Review of Theories & Treatments." *Psychoneuroendocrinology*, 2, 1977.

Steinmann, M., "The Progesterone Controversy." *Contemporary OB/GYN*, 11, 1978.

Sutherland, H., and Stewart, I., "A Critical Analysis of the Premenstrual Syndrome." *Lancet*, 1, 1965.

"The Tampax Report," conducted by Ruder Finn & Rotman, 1981.

Vollman, Rudolf F., *The Menstrual Cycle*. W. B. Saunders Co., 1977.

"Ways to Chart Your Fertility Pattern," Planned Parenthood Federation of America, Inc., November 1980.

Weideger, Paula, *Menstruation and Menopause*. Alfred A. Knopf, 1980.

"What Is Premenstrual Syndrome?" PMS Action, Inc., 1981.

Wender, Paul H., and Klein, Donald F., *Mind, Mood and Medicine*. Farrar, Straus & Giroux, Inc., 1981.

Williams, Robert H. (ed.), *Textbook of Endocrinology*. W. B. Saunders Co., 1968.

"Women's Curse: A General Internist's Approach to Common Menstrual Problems," *The Western Journal of Medicine*, January 1983.

"Women's Views Study," Mark Clements Research, Inc., conducted for *Glamour*, 1983.

"You Needn't Suffer Premenstrual Tension," *Today's Living*, November 1982.

INDEX

Index